J. Graves 495

From Hook To Table

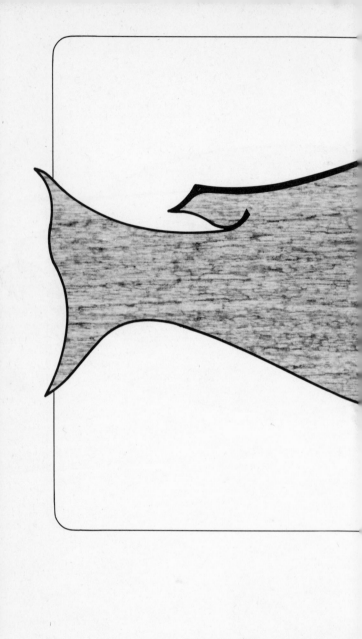

From Hook To Table

Vic Dunaway

Macmillan Publishing Co., Inc.
NEW YORK
Collier Macmillan Publishers
LONDON

To my old and good friend Dan Schooler, who may be the only person who likes to eat fish more than I do.

Macmillan Publishing Co., Inc.
866 Third Avenue, New York, N. Y. 10022
Collier-Macmillan Canada Ltd.

Library of Congress Cataloging in Publication Data

Dunaway, Vic.
    From hook to table.

    1. Cookery (Fish) 2. Fish handling. I. Title.
TX747.D86   641.3'92   73-14110
ISBN 0-02-533900-1

FIRST PRINTING 1974

Printed in the United States of America

Contents

Foreword   vii
On the Water   1
Fish Cleaning and Dressing   7
Cold-Storing and Freezing Fish   45
Basic Cooking Methods   59
Cooking Fish Outdoors   69
Recipes, Simple and Fancy   85
Guide to Hook-and-Line Table Fish   113
Calorie Listing   139
Index   143

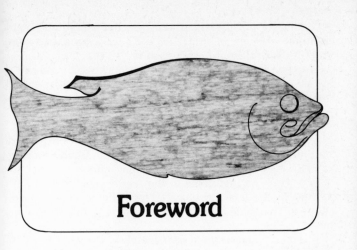

Foreword

Perhaps no other food is so dependent on "freshness" for optimum enjoyment as is fish. Beef or game or almost any other type of red meat may be improved by aging—that is, deliberately allowing the meat, under controlled conditions, to develop a flavor which is riper than that of the fresh meat. But with fish, the aim always is to maintain that delicate, fresh-caught taste; to prevent, if at all possible, even the slightest hint of ripeness.

Many kinds of fish, if properly frozen, can be eaten months after they are caught and still taste perfectly fresh. Yet the very same kinds might just as easily develop a disagreeably strong flavor only a day—even hours—after being pulled from the water. The difference, of course, lies in how well they are cared for.

All too many anglers, whether in haste or ignorance, take proper care of their catch at some stages between hook and table, but not at others. All steps are crucial. A fish that is tainted will not lose its rancidity in the freezer, no matter how well you wrap and store it. Nor will a fish gently handled on the water and lovingly carried home on a dry bed of ice be any less likely to freezer-burn if sloppily frozen.

Oddly, a lot of fishermen who treat the handling of their fish quite casually show far too much concern about cooking. It's not unusual for a person to feel that every species of fish has its own special ways of being cooked, and must be prepared just-so. These misguided souls might spend hours looking up a recipe for, say, bluefish, after they have refused to spend five minutes making sure their catch is well-iced and drained for the drive home.

Anyone who follows the few simple procedures explained in the chapters on cooking should have little trouble making a tasty dish out of any fish he might catch—whether he can or can't find its name in the family cookbook.

And in the more involved recipes offered here, it's not the fish that might be difficult to prepare, but what goes on it.

For maximum usefulness of the book, I suggest you first look up your fish in the listings in Chapter 7. There you will get skeleton suggestions on how to dress the fish and how best to cook it. Then you can consult Chapter 2 for cleaning instructions in step-by-step detail, and from there go to Chapter 4 for basic cooking procedures.

Almost always, there is a wide choice of possibilities for any food fish. It's up to you to decide whether you want simply fried, broiled or baked fish, or want to try one of the more than 50 recipes in Chapter 6.

For outdoor cooking, look at Chapter 5.

But for all that advice, you probably won't be happy with your meal unless you pay careful attention to the proper handling of your catch, as outlined in Chapters 1 and 3.

From Hook To Table

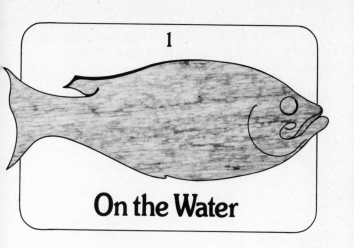

On the Water

Understandably enough, a fisherman's main concern while he's on the water is to catch fish. Any matter of less pressing import—even eating lunch—is apt to be postponed as long as possible, or at least as long as there are good-looking spots to be cast to and the angler is not too exhausted to lift his arm.

But in fishing, as in every other pursuit, there are necessary chores which demand attention. Time must be made for paddling and rigging and anchoring and sharpening hooks. And for the millions of fishermen who enjoy eating their fish almost as much as catching them, time must also be carefully devoted to the few small but vital requirements of proper care which will assure getting the catch home in a fresh and flavorful condition.

Angling is primarily a warm-weather sport, and so your immediate aim must be to hold down the natural rise in temperature of fish after they leave the water. Obviously, in those few cases where the air temperature is as low as, or lower than, the water temperature (ice fishing, for instance, or certain other kinds of winter fishing), the problem is not so serious, and may not exist at all; but in the overall fishing picture, such cases are far in the minority.

1

One good way to hold off deterioration is to keep the fish alive as long as possible. With most freshwater fish (notable exceptions being trout and salmon) and with many saltwater fish as well, you can either string the fish and return them to the water, or else deposit them in a fish bag or basket which is held in the water, and be confident that they will remain frisky for some time.

STRINGERS

Stringers are available in two basic styles. One is simply a cord fitted at one end with a rigid point and at the other with a ring. You slip the point under the gill of a fish and out its mouth. Then you pull the stringer all the way through until the ring is just outside the gill. Now, by running the point through the ring and tightening it, you secure the first fish to the stringer. With all others, you simply run the point through gill and mouth.

The second common type is the chain stringer, which features individual safety-pin type clips for every fish you put on it. Though the chain stringer can be used for other species, it is most popular among bass fishermen—its eight or ten clips representing the daily bag limit for bass in most states. The best method for affixing a bass to one of the clips is to run the open point of the clip through *both* lips of the bass.

When stringing a fish you should handle it as little as possible and get the stringer into the water at once. Be sure that the other end of the stringer is firmly fastened to boat or bank. This may sound like unnecessary advice, and indeed it should be, but many an unhappy fisherman has lost a good string of fish through carelessness in this regard.

So long as the stringer remains submerged, your fish have a good chance of staying alive. But it's a rare angler who doesn't move from spot to spot during a day's fishing. Chances are your catch will survive short periods of transport lying on the deck, but if you anticipate a long haul, it's best to deposit the string in a pail of water. In either event, don't forget to put the stringer overside as soon as you stop.

A stringer can safely be left in the water while you paddle

or slow-troll. As a matter of fact, slow movement undoubtedly adds to the stringer-life of your fish. But when you motor at even a medium speed, the stringer must be taken aboard.

Fish bags and baskets have the same function as stringers, their purpose being to keep your fish alive and in the water. Many boats are fitted with live-wells, and while such wells are mainly for bait, your fish can be kept in them too, so long as they don't become overcrowded. Note, however, that it's a rare live-well which recirculates water copiously enough to keep larger fish alive for any great length of time.

Whether you use a stringer, bag or live-well, you must keep a steady check on the fish and quickly make other arrangements for any that die. Dead fish are apt to spoil more rapidly in the water than out of it.

It's a good idea to remove any casualties from stringer or bag at once. If you don't have an ice chest, simply put them in a shady spot where there is free circulation of air, or cover loosely with a damp rag or moss or other vegetation. The dampness will help keep them cool by evaporation, and also helps prevent the surface drying that would make them more difficult to dress later on.

ICE CHESTS

Anyone who fishes from a boat should by all means take along a portable ice chest and a supply of ice. These chests are available in such an array of sizes that you can find one which will fit even the smallest boat without crowding. Nor is it much trouble to carry along an ice chest when you fish from dock or bridge. Folks who do their fishing afoot obviously cannot lug along a box of ice, but unless it's only a short drive home, they should at least keep an ice chest in the car.

The surest and easiest method for taking care of a fresh-caught fish is to deposit it directly in an ice chest. Thereafter, the only thing to worry about until time to dress your catch is that the box stays reasonably well drained, and, of course, that it remains shut except when you must put something in or take something out.

Often, however, it is impractical to carry along an ice

chest for the exclusive purpose of holding your catch. One chest may have to serve double duty as a repository for cold drinks, and in this case you still make effective use of a stringer. Keep your fish on the stringer so long as they remain frisky, but if a fish dies, transfer it to the ice chest. To avoid contact with your drinks or lunch, place the fish in a plastic bag first. Or keep your lunch in a tight container, and don't worry about the drinks. A rinse and a wipe will remove all traces of fishy taste or aroma from bottle or can.

At trip's end, of course, you put all your fish on ice for the ride home. However, if you prefer to dress your fish before leaving the waterside, here are a few other pointers which should be followed.

With dressed fish, special care should be taken to make sure that the fish don't sit in water which has melted from the ice. Fish flesh that comes into contact with water— even ice water—can quickly become soft and unappetizing. Drain the chest thoroughly before packing your dressed fish. And if you have to drive a long way, plan one or more stops to drain the chest en route.

With filleted fish, rather than fish which are merely scaled and drawn, it is even more important to keep them dry in the ice chest. It is best to put the fillets in a plastic bag first. If plastic bags aren't available, cover the ice with several thicknesses of newspaper and place the fillets on top of that.

TROUT AND SALMON

It has been mentioned that trout and salmon are not to be spiked on stringers. The proper handling of those fish seems almost ritualistic, yet the ritual is a practical one, designed to keep these delicate table species at their peak of appearance and flavor.

As soon as a trout or salmon is caught it should be killed quickly with a blow on the head or, in the case of smaller specimens, by breaking the back, just behind the head, with your hands. Ideally, the fish should then be dressed at once, but chances are you're anxious to cast again. So lay the fish aside and dress it at the very first

4

break. The fish should be placed in a creel of wicker or mesh (so air can circulate), or else placed in a shady spot in the boat or on the bank.

As soon as you can get to it, slit the fish and remove the entrails and gills, as well as the blood-line along the backbone (the procedure is illustrated in Chapter 2). The fish should then be wrapped in a dry rag, or dry grass, and returned to the creel. Naturally, you don't put king-sized salmon in a creel, but you still dress as soon as possible, then keep them in a cool and *dry* place.

Part of the ritual, with small trout especially, is to keep individual fish from coming into contact with each other, since any point of contact will result in a blemish. It doesn't harm the taste or texture—just the sensitivity of some trout fishermen.

The reason trout and salmon are killed so quickly is to prevent flapping around with resultant damage to the surface appearance. A lot of people refer to such damage as "bruises" and swear that every bruise impugns the flavor. I really don't think the quality of the fish is harmed by bumps and jolts, but the appearance definitely is, and to many, that is a goodly part of a trout dinner.

On the other hand, there is no debate about the effect of water on a dressed trout. If the trout must be washed, rinse it lightly and wipe at once. Preferably, you should not wash, but wipe with a damp rag to remove any foreign substances.

Trout and salmon which are put on ice should be even more carefully bagged or wrapped than other species.

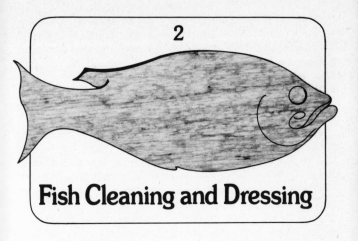

2

Fish Cleaning and Dressing

Perhaps cleaning fish will never be looked upon as one of man's great recreational delights, but at least the task becomes less objectionable if three basic rules are followed: (1) keep the right tools handy; (2) clean the fish in a place selected for maximum ease and convenience; (3) familiarize yourself with any of the different cleaning techniques you're likely to need—and practice them.

Often the only tool needed is a knife, but it must be a good one—and sharp. The most useful will be a fillet knife with six-inch blade. Many models are available on fishing tackle counters, and with stainless blades they range in price from about $1.50 to perhaps $5.00. Most of the lower-priced knives work well, but are apt to need more frequent sharpening than the more expensive ones, and consequently will have a shorter life.

Knives with carbon steel blades work just as well and are sharpened more quickly: however, they do rust.

It's advisable to keep one of the six-inch fillet knives in your tackle kit, and an identical one at home. And it's not a bad idea to keep *two* in the tackle box. Just in case your fishing buddy can't produce a knife of his own at cleaning time, you can politely offer him one of yours so he'll be able to help with the cleaning.

If you fish often for stream trout or panfish, you'll find a smaller knife more convenient, even though a six-incher will do the job. For small-fish dressing you can use either a good pocket knife or a smaller version of the six-inch fillet knife—one with a three- or four-inch blade.

Other cleaning tools which may well come in handy—depending on where you fish, and for what—are a scaler and a pair of pliers.

And it almost goes without saying that a sharpening stone should always be close at hand. Again, try to keep one in your tackle box and another at home, for those times when you're unable to clean your fish on the water.

Obviously, you could drag your tools out of the tackle box for home cleaning, which would be perfectly all right so long as you're the infallible type who always remembers to put them back. Unfortunately, I'm not. Nor are any of my fishing pals.

A waterside table saves as much time and inconvenience as the right tools. Most marinas and fish camps do provide fish-cleaning facilities—a wooden table of the appropriate height, complete with handy water supply. But even without those, you'll normally find it easier to clean fish on location than to bring them home and do it.

Fish scales fly hither and yon as you scrape them off, and your wife may take a dim view of scales speckling her walls and ceiling. Also, there is a disposal problem in the average city home—particularly the many without daily garbage pickup.

If for any reason you must dress your fish at home, here are some hints that should help. When scaling fish, hold them in a sink full of water so the scales won't fly about. Then, for gutting and beheading, place numerous thicknesses of newspaper on a counter top. As the mess grows, keep wrapping it in a few layers of paper and setting it aside. This not only avoids a single big pile of garbage, but also allows you a new clean surface from time to time as you go along.

When filleting fish at home (rather than scaling and dressing), place the pad of newspaper sheets atop a cutting

8

board and, again, wrap the refuse at intervals as you find necessary.

As each fish (or fillet) leaves the cleaning surface, it should be placed, without rinsing, in a dry sink or dry, clean pail. When the whole job is finished, rinse all the fish under cold running water and then immediately prepare them for cold-storing or freezing as described in Chapter 3.

Several factors must be considered in determing how you wish to dress your fish. One, obviously, is size. You wouldn't try to stuff and bake an average-size bluegill. The selected method of cooking is another consideration. When you bring home a fat striped bass, say, or a red snapper, or a four-pound smallmouth bass, you'll have a decision to make. Should you prepare the fish whole for baking, or remove the fillets for frying or broiling?

Such fish as large salmon and king mackerel are normally steaked. But in smaller sizes, they could be either steaked or filleted, according to your own preference.

Once you make a choice as to the end product desired, proceed with the task of dressing, as described in the illustrated instructions which follow.

DRESSING PANFISH

"Panfish" is a catchall term for any edible fish, from fresh water or salt, which is so small that it's normally cooked in a nearly-whole condition. Naturally, the entrails must be removed, and usually the head is lopped off as well. Some people, however, prefer to leave the head on. In that case, the gills should be cut out. The majority of panfish also require scaling. Some, such as stream trout and saltwater pompano, need not be scaled. The list of edible fish in this book makes note of those kinds which need no scaling, but if any doubt persists, it really won't hurt any of them to undergo a mild scraping.

1. Since you'll usually be dressing a lot of panfish at once, you should use a scaling device that's fast and efficient. The patented scaler shown here is excellent. There are several other very good ones available. Or you can use a knife (preferably dull) or a spoon—whatever suits you best.

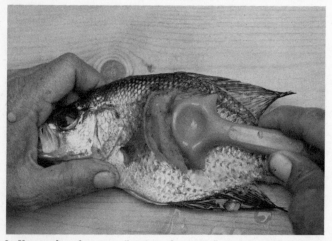

2. You scale, of course, "against the grain," or from tail to head. Be sure to get the scales close to the dorsal and anal fins.

3. Pay extra attention to spots that might be overlooked if you are in too big a hurry—top and bottom surfaces, as shown, and the "throat" area.

4. Cut off the head. Some like to cut the pectoral fins off with it, as shown. Others prefer to cut closer behind the gills and leave the pectorals.

5. Slit belly and remove entrails.

6. Panfish is ready for the pan. Dorsal and ventral fins could be cut out (see how in *Preparing a Large Fish for Baking,* p. 15), but it's a lot of trouble and not really necessary, because the fins are easily removed after cooking (see Chapter 5).

Dressing Panfish, Hand-Held

Here's an alternate system for dressing panfish when no cleaning table or flat surface is available. Use it at streamside or lakeside when preparing fish for a cookout.

7. Hold fish in hand and, with the blade of a pocket knife held vertically, scrape off the scales. Turn fish over and scrape other side. Take care to remove scales as well from any top and bottom surfaces. Since scales flake from fresh panfish without much effort, you are not apt to cut yourself, but you obviously must be careful.

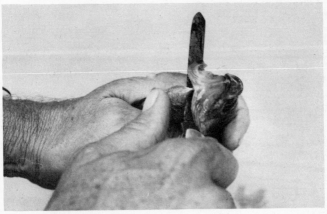

8. After scaling, insert knife blade through gills and cut through the "throat" connection.

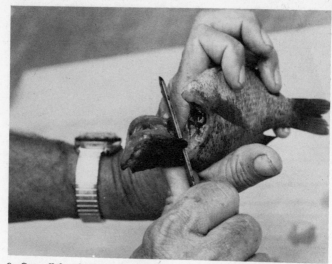

9. Cut off head. You can now remove entrails either by making a slit in the belly cavity, or by inserting a finger into the cavity from the front and pulling them out.

10. Rinse well, and panfish is ready for mealing and cooking.

14

PREPARING LARGE FISH FOR BAKING

Procedures for dressing a larger fish, which you plan to bake, are essentially the same as for panfish. But it's a bigger job that will take more effort and elbow room. You may also wish to remove the dorsal and anal fins. If you do, be sure not to cut them off at the surface, but follow the pictures carefully so that connective bones are removed as well. Simply cutting off the fins may make the fish look neat, but leaves extra and completely unnecessary bones.

You may also cut off the tail, but there is no real reason to do so—unless it overlaps your baking pan.

Preparing a Large Fish for Baking

1. The first step is to scale the fish. This can be a pretty tough job. Your best tool, again, is the patented scaler, although a sturdy tablespoon will do the trick. As with panfish, take care that all scales are removed from dorsal and belly surfaces, as well as from the sides.

15

2. Remove the head. Some like to leave the head on, and if you prefer to do so, be sure to cut out the gills. It can be a rough job to cut through the spine of a fairly large fish. It may help to first cut through the "throat" as shown in the picture, then grasp the head from the underside and pull it outward and toward the back to break the spine. The ordinary knife will then easily cut through.

3. Slit the belly from vent to throat. A little effort will be needed to split the fin.

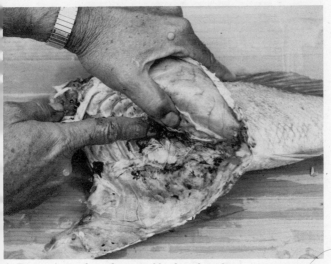

4. Remove entrails and scrape blood pockets from spine area.

5. At this stage the fish could be ready. The fins can be left on because they're easily pulled out after cooking. But if you prefer to remove them now, here's how:

6. Keeping knife blade flat, make a rather deep cut the length of the dorsal fin. Turn fish and make the same cut along the other side of the dorsal.

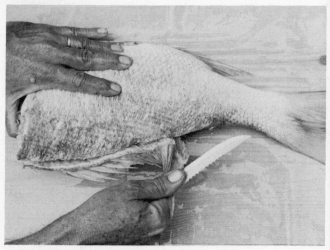

7. Using the knife to help grip, grasp the dorsal fin at the tail end and pull firmly toward the head end. The fin and all connecting bones will come out.

8. Do exactly the same thing as in steps 6 and 7 with the smaller anal (lower) fin. No need to remove the other fins (pectoral and ventral) since these are attached to large rigid bones rather than troublesome small ones. This is your fish, ready for baking.

DRESSING TROUT AND SALMON

These fish should be field-dressed as soon as they're caught, or very shortly thereafter. See Chapter 1.

Dressing Trout and Salmon

1. Make a slit the entire length of the belly from vent to gills, and cut the "throat" where gills are joined to head on underside.

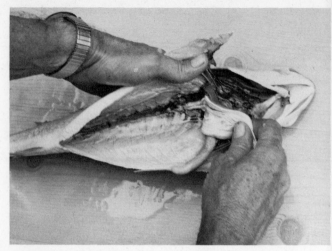

2. Remove entrails, and pull out the gills.

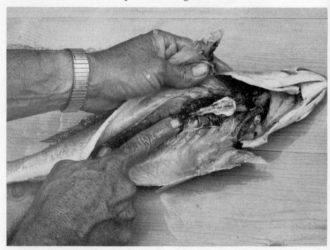

3. With forefinger, work out the bloodline along the backbone. Trout should now be wiped clean. Trout scales are so small they can be ignored. Therefore, this field-dressing system (see Chapter 1) is all the cleaning that's needed. Of course, with larger salmon or trout, you will wish to steak or fillet before cooking.

STEAKING

When should a fish be steaked instead of filleted? There's no rigid rule on this, but these tips may help.

(1) Follow custom. Halibut, salmon, king mackerel and swordfish are usually sold in steaks. So are other species from area to area. Anglers generally follow the custom with their own catches.

(2) Appearance. You may simply "like the looks" of a broiled steak over those of a fillet cut from the same fish.

(3) Variable size. You can cut fish steaks to any thickness—using thin steaks for quick recipes, thick ones for slower cooking with sauces and extra trimmings.

In addition, there is the most basic practical reason of all for steaking—when you have a fish so large that its fillets would be too thick for convenient cooking or handling.

To prepare a fish for steaking, proceed as described for dressing whole fish—scale, remove the head and remove the entrails. Then, with the carcass lying flat on a cutting board, simply make a straight-down cut, very much like slicing a loaf of bread. Of course, there are no bones in a loaf of bread. The backbone of your fish may or may not cause trouble.

Sometimes, with fairly small fish or with certain species, your knife will slice right through the bone with only a little extra effort—especially if you happen to hit between the vertebrae. But if the bone resists your knife, simply cut through the flesh until you hit the bone, then take care of the bone with a kitchen saw, frozen food knife or cleaver. Once the bone is severed, pick up your slicing knife once more and cut through the lower flesh.

Near the tail end of the carcass, your steaks may become so small that they aren't worth fooling with. You can either preserve the tail portion for baking or boiling in one large chunk, or you can fillet the remaining meat from both sides of the bone—just like filleting a whole fish.

Steaking

For steaking, fish should first be prepared exactly as for baking—cut off the head, remove entrails, scale if necessary, and remove the fins. Should you leave the dorsal and anal fins on the fish, you'll have bothersome small bones in the steaks.

King mackerel, mackerel, salmon and some other fish have no scales, or scales so small they can be ignored.

After you dress the fish, simply cut off steaks of the desired thickness by cutting straight down—much like slicing a loaf of bread. Use a kitchen saw, serrated knife or cleaver to cut through the spine, if necessary.

Steaks usually are cut three-quarters of an inch to one inch thick.

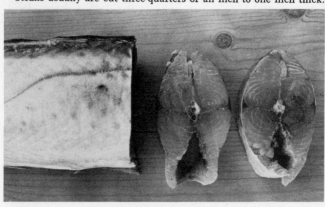

HOW TO FILLET AND SKIN, SYSTEM 1

This is the easiest and fastest of all fish-cleaning methods, and suitable for the great majority of angler catches. The product is a slab of solid, boneless or nearly boneless, fish flesh. Both skin and scales are removed simultaneously. If you prefer to scale the fish and leave the skin on each fillet, that's up to you. Skin adds something to the taste of many species, but in others it imparts a strong, disagreeable flavor. Consult the list of fish in this book for guidelines on this matter, but remember that even in species which don't really require it, removing the skin means only a slightly milder flavor.

Many fishermen may never think of filleting any fish under, say, one pound in weight. But there are times when you may well wish to consider filleting large bluegills, small mangrove snapper, or other species which normally are treated as panfish. Such types will produce quite small fillets, of course, but if you have a great many of them—enough, at least, to feed the number of people you have in mind—you'll find them delicious.

Outsize bluegills or other sunfish, caught from still or muddy water, often have a strong flavor much like that of a largemouth bass taken from the same water. If so, filleting and skinning will remove it.

How to Fillet and Skin, System 1

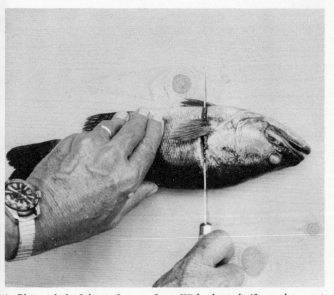

1. Place whole fish on firm surface. With sharp knife, make a cut straight down, just behind the pectoral fin and all the way to the backbone.

2. Turn the knife edge toward the tail, until blade is flat against backbone. Keeping knife flat, work with a slight sawing motion all the way to the tail, thus removing the entire fillet. The rib bones remain with the fillet.

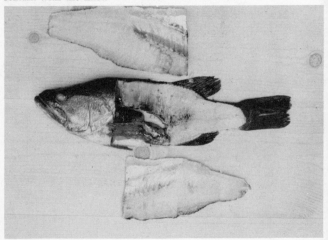

3. Repeat on other side, and you have both fillets, ready to skin. Rest of fish can be discarded. Or you can remove head and entrails and keep the backbone.

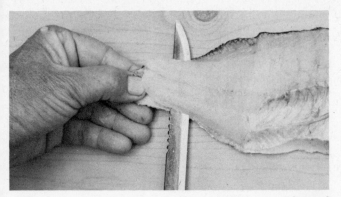

4. Starting at tail end, work knife edge carefully between skin and fillet. Grasp tail-end of skin with thumb and fingers, as shown. Keeping knife almost flat—but with edge pointed *very slightly* downward—pull on the skin while you work knife with a slight scissors motion toward the head end. You should exert more pressure pulling the skin than pushing the knife.

5. The skin should separate from the fillet in one piece, as at top. The fillet, bottom, still has the rib cage intact, but you can now easily cut this away, leaving one boneless piece of meat.

HOW TO SKIN AND FILLET, SYSTEM 2

The end result of this method is the same as that of the preceding system, but the order is reversed. You remove the skin first, and then cut off the fillet. Why two different systems for doing the same thing? Mainly because you'll run into an occasional species of fish—dolphin is a prime example—which just doesn't surrender its hide easily after the fillet is removed.

There's also the matter of personal viewpoint. This system is widely used, although for most fish I prefer the previous one.

How to Skin and Fillet, System 2

1. Make a shallow cut along the dorsal surface at the base of the fin, from just back of the head to the tail.

2. Make a shallow diagonal cut as shown, from the forward end of the top cut to the belly near the vent. Then cut along bottom side to the tail.

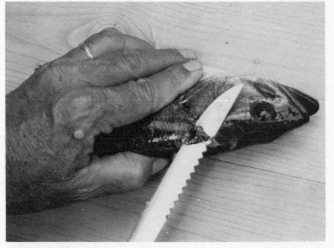

3. Use the knife blade to pry up a bit of skin at angle of the two cuts behind the head.

4. Grasp the piece of skin between thumb and finger. Holding head firmly with other hand, pull and the skin will come off in one piece. With large fish, you might have to use pliers to pull the skin off.

5. Now you can carefully trim the fillet away from the backbone. Let the knife edge slide around the rib cage and you'll have a completely boneless fillet. Proceed exactly the same way on the other side.

THE DOUBLE FILLET

Both fillets taken from the same fish can be left attached on the underside, providing a double fillet, sometimes called a "butterfly" fillet.

There are several standard uses for a double fillet. One is planking—that is, tacking or pinning the meat to a wooden plank or shingle, then propping the shingle at the edge of an open fire for campfire broiling.

Many like a double fillet for home use. They spread a stuffing atop one side, fold the other side over it and bake. They could do the same thing with the same two fillets, whether attached or not, but I suppose there is some *chic* involved.

To produce a double fillet, you must leave the skin on, since that's what holds it together. So, obviously, you have to scale the fish for home baking. For planked fish, however, it's best to leave the scales intact, and when chow time arrives, you fork the meat away from the skin.

The Double Fillet

1. First, scale fish and cut off head of pectoral fin. Remove entrails.

2. Starting at head end, position knife flat against backbone, then cut toward rear—cutting through rib bones, but taking care not to cut through belly skin. When you reach the vent, however, push knife point through bottom skin, then finish cutting the fillet to the tail.

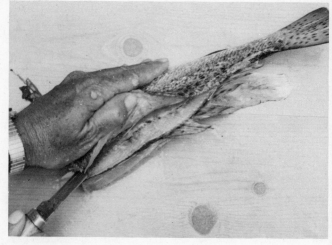

3. Turn fish and follow the same procedure on the other side.

4. This is the double fillet—great for planking or for stuffing and baking.

FILLETING EXTRA-LARGE FISH

If a fish "fits the knife," then slicing off each fillet is routine. But with an unusually large fish, you'll have to go about things a little differently. One approach, obviously, would be to get a longer knife. Another is to cut as far as you can with your short blade, then raise the filleted portion up and away as you make succeedingly deeper cuts until finally the whole side is sliced off.

Now, of course, the fillet is still too wide to permit skinning in the normal manner. Attack this problem, as shown in the illustrations, by making two or more small fillets out of a single large one.

An alternate approach is to use System 2 and remove the skin before tackling the fillet. On a big fish, however, you'll need a lot of muscle. This way is better.

Filleting Extra-Large Fish

Although you cannot slice off the fillet with one continuous stroke of the knife as you can with smaller fish, it really isn't too difficult to fillet a fish which is wider than the length of your knife blade.

1. Make a vertical cut to the backbone, just behind the gill, then slice through the skin from the vertical cut all the way to the tail, along the dorsal (top) surface.

2. Lift the edge of the fillet and continue slicing it away from the bone.

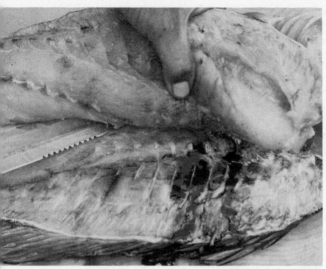

3. Keep lifting and slicing until you reach the skin on the underside, then cut through the skin and remove the fillet.

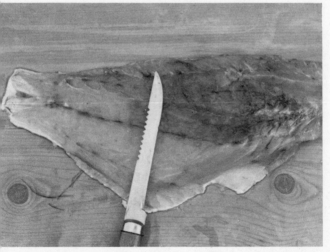

4. Now, of course, the fillet is still too wide to allow skinning in the manner described previously, so. . .

5. ... you simply make the fillet "fit the knife" by cutting it in half lengthwise, along the obvious center line.

6. Now each half can be skinned as if it were a single fillet.

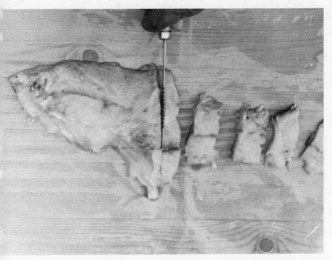

7. The final step is to cut each half-fillet into serving-size pieces. Or, it can be left whole for broiling or baking.

BUTCHERING GIANT FISH

Should you set about skinning and cutting up a really huge catch—such as a giant sea bass, shark or billfish weighing several hundred pounds—the task could be as challenging as butchering a big-game animal. If faced with such a chore, you can take either of two approaches:

(1) Hang the fish by putting a rope through its gill and winching it up to a stout support. Then cut through the skin all around one side, and with laborious effort, tug the skin away. It will have to be yanked and peeled back little by little, and probably helped along by constant and careful knife-work between skin and meat. And then, of course, you'll have to do the same with the other side. Once the skin is removed, you cut the meat from the bone in pieces, rather than in one immense fillet.

(2) Leave the fish on the ground and cut away the meat chunk by chunk, skin and all, and then skin each of the chunks later. Since the skin is apt to be leather-tough, you

should use a heavy, sharp knife—and extra precautions must be taken to keep from cutting yourself. The knife blade might tend to slip, and you'll be making a lot of cuts.

Giant bluefin tuna, marlin, swordfish, mako shark and other big-game fish can be treated as described in the preceding paragraph—should you decide to eat them instead of releasing or mounting them. All are quite good, although only the swordfish is famous as food.

You have the option of steaking swordfish, marlin and shark. But steaking those giants can be an even tougher project. They do it in commercial houses, but they have the equipment for it.

Butchering Giant Fish

Big-game fish aren't often thought of as table fare by sportsmen. With the exception of swordfish, these prizes are more often sent to the taxidermist than to the kitchen. And anglers who fish with some regularity for big game release most of their catches.

Still, quite a few marlin, sailfish and giant tuna are killed and brought to dock for one reason or another, and should be utilized for food more often than they are. Marlin are at least as good as swordfish. Sailfish make a great delicacy when smoked. Thin slices cut from chunks of giant tuna can be pan-broiled, and taste much like baby beef.

36

Obviously, these huge fish do not lend themselves to ordinary cleaning-table treatment. Perhaps the best way to go about claiming the meat is simply to take a large, sharp knife and carve chunks from the thick meaty areas—beginning just behind the gills, and extending all the way to the tail.

The large chunks can be baked, or cut into thinner portions for broiling, frying or smoking.

Take whatever meat you can use, and invite anyone and everyone else on the dock to sharpen their knives and help themselves.

SKINNING CATFISH

Catfish always should be skinned, whether they're of panfish size or lunkers which will afterward be filleted or chunked. The skin is tough, but thin and slippery, and the procedure is different from those used for scaly fishes.

Skinning Catfish

1. A board with a nail driven through it at an angle is extremely helpful in skinning catfish, especially if you have a lot to skin.

2. Make a cut through the skin from one side, across the top, to the other side, just back of the head.

3. Impale the head of the fish on the nail. Grasp skin at the cut with pliers and pull toward tail.

4. Skin usually will come off in one piece. Sometimes, however, it will separate along the dorsal surface. This means only that you'll have to grip and pull a second time. No bother.

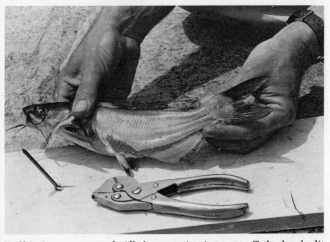

5. Skin is now removed. All that remains is to cut off the head, slit the belly and remove the entrails. If a small strip of skin remains on the belly, pull it off with pliers before slitting. Small catfish can be fried whole. Larger ones can be filleted easily after cleaning.

BONING SHAD

Shad roe is a famous delicacy. So is shad—even though all too many anglers discard the fish, or give it away, because they don't want to tackle all the bones that are buried inside the meat.

Boning shad is relatively simple, but few people know how it's done. For many years it was considered a secret art. The few who knew the process didn't like to tell even their closest pals.

Boning Shad

Shad roe is a famous delicacy. The fillets also rank among the best in all fishdom, but—oh—those bones! Some anglers enjoy shad so much that they're willing to battle the bones, bite by bite. All too many folks, however, keep only the roe, and discard or give away the shad. Shad *can* be completely boned. Here's how:

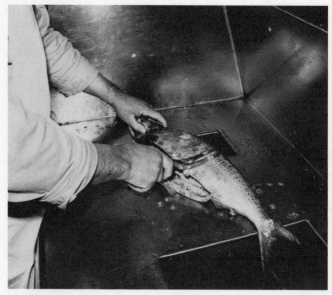

1. Slit the belly carefully to avoid puncturing roe. Remove roe and entrails. Scale shad and cut off head.

2. To remove fillet, work edge of sharp knife through skin along length of dorsal surface...

3. ...then lift up fillet and continue cutting close to backbone. Let knife slide over the top of rib-cage bones rather than cut through them. Or you can go ahead and slice off the entire fillet, rib cage and all, then cut away the entire rib cage as described previously under *How to Fillet and Skin*.

41

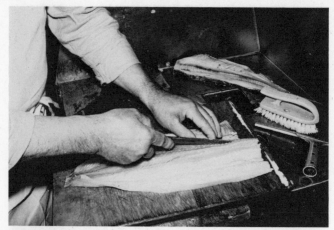

4. Lay fillet skin side down. The "extra" bones in a shad fillet are located in two rows, each running the length of the fillet about one inch on either side of the center line. To get at these bones, make a lengthwise cut about one-half inch from the center line on either side.

5. Insert knife point in one of the lengthwise cuts and work it underneath the bone, prying up slightly until you can get a grip on the bone with your fingers.

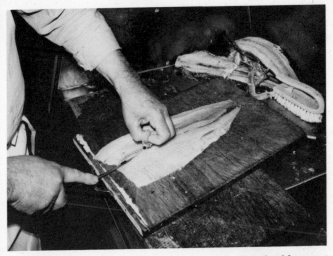

6. Now pull gently, and you can work the entire length of bone out of the fillet.

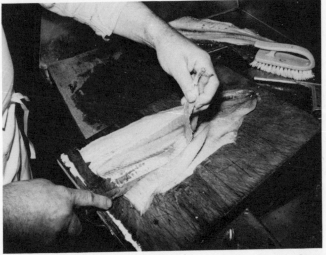

7. But don't forget that each fillet has *two* strips of bone. Go to the other side of the center line and work the second set of bones out in the same way. The fillet is now boneless and ready for broiling.

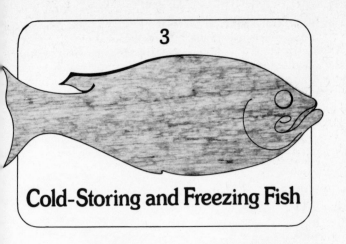

3

Cold-Storing and Freezing Fish

As soon as you get home from a fishing trip, you should make sure that your fish are taken care of before doing any other chores. Even before you wash the boat or sit down to dinner, at least check the ice chest. If plenty of ice is left, and proper drainage seen to, you can safely postpone refrigerating or freezing—perhaps even until the following morning. Just be sure the ice will last (or add more), and open the drain plug.

Should you wish to keep fish for several days without freezing them, you can manage it in either of two ways. A small amount of fish can be wrapped and stored in the coldest part of your refrigerator for up to three days—particularly in a covered meat keeper where the temperature is not apt to drop drastically with frequent opening of the refrigerator door. If you're trying to hold a larger quantity of fish than the refrigerator can efficiently accommodate, keep them in your portable ice chest, well packed with crushed ice.

But remember that the chest must be checked every few hours. If you're away at work, assign the chore to someone else once or twice during the day. A modern chest, well-insulated with plastic foam, will probably hold the ice well for several hours, anyway—depending on the ratio of fish to ice which it contains. The scheduled checks, however are as much for drainage as for ice supply. It's common for the drain to get stopped up. So run a pencil or screw driver blade into the drain at every check to assure that there's no blockage.

Drain Ice Chest

Water should be drained from ice chest regularly when fish are stored or transported on ice. Especially with dressed fish, water contact causes loss of color and flavor, and also imparts a "mushy" texture.

Personally, I prefer to freeze my fish, even if I plan on using them within a few days. But I know several persons who often catch their fish one weekend and keep them in ice chests until the next, when they host a fish-fry.

For different reasons, fish kept either in a refrigerator or an ice chest must be protected with an air-tight or water-tight cover. In the refrigerator, fish dries out so rapidly that it can lose quality within an hour or so. Long contact with water, on the other hand, tends to make the flesh soft and robs it of flavor—hence the constant harping on plastic bags and drainage for iced fish.

I seldom refrigerate fresh fish unless I plan to cook it the next day. Then I cut it into frying-size pieces, put the pieces in a bowl, and cover the bowl with plastic wrap. Or, if it is a large fish which I plan to bake, I wrap the whole thing in foil or heavy wrapping paper—as carefully as I would for freezing.

Holding Fish in Refrigerator

When dressed and ready for the table, fish may be held in the refrigerator for up to three days without losing quality—so long as they are well covered. Uncovered fish dry out quickly in cold air, and can impart "fishy" odors to other foods. So cover refrigerated fish, even if you plan to use it a couple of hours later. Large fish can be wrapped in foil or freezer paper, as for freezing. Small portions can be placed in a bowl and covered with plastic wrap, as shown. The wrap will adhere to the sides of the bowl and provide tight protection against air.

HOW TO FREEZE FISH

When properly packaged and kept in a freezer which can be depended upon to freeze them quickly and keep them frozen solidly, many kinds of fish can be kept for a year—and they still taste fresh when served.

Such long-term freezing can be accomplished with the lean types of fish, characterized by firm, white meat, and little or no red or dark streaks. Examples include freshwater bass and panfish, saltwater grouper, snook, flounder and many others.

Fat or oily fishes, such as mackerel, bluefish, mullet and salmon do not have nearly so long a freezer life, because the oils in their flesh tend to go rancid. Until I hit upon the coffee-can freezing method, which will be described shortly, I found that mullet and mackerel developed a rancid taste in the freezer within a week or two. But now I enjoy them up to three months after freezing.

If you're not sure whether a particular kind of fish is lean or fat, the rule of thumb is that the fat ones usually have an obviously dark-tinted flesh—pink in the case of salmon and trout; grayish or reddish in mackerel, blues and most tunas.

As mentioned above, the meat of lean fish is white, although there may be patches of red. Even with these, best freezing results will be obtained if you trim away the red parts, as these are blood streaks which may go rancid.

Everyone knows that fish should be wrapped well before freezing to avoid drying out (called "freezer burn"). Dried spots are not harmful, but the dried areas themselves are tough and tasteless, and when you see spots of freezer-burn, you can almost be sure that the rest of the fish will have, at best, an unfresh taste.

The very best way of protecting fish from freezer burn is to freeze them within a block of ice. And there are refinements even here. Long ago, I used to put fish in an ice-cube tray, fill the tray with water, freeze the whole thing, and then remove the frozen block, wrap it in freezer paper and return it to the freezer. Later I graduated to

48

lastic milk cartons—depositing fillets or panfish therein,
lling with water and folding down the top. This was a
reat improvement, but neither procedure is nearly so
andy, fast or completely protective as the device I now
se—a metal coffee can.

In my household there is seldom a shortage of coffee
ans, and we even have them in two sizes, since we buy
egular coffee in two-pound containers, and decaffeinated
offee in the one-pound can.

If you're a fish-loving angler who drinks instant coffee,
t's worth going back to home-brewed just to get the cans.
have found that, in addition to their sheer convenience,
hey keep frozen fish fresh-tasting far longer than any
ther container or wrap.

Two reasons undoubtedly contribute to the long freezer
fe. First, freezing takes place much faster because of the
netal's conductivity. Second, the fish is doubly guarded—
y solid metal and by ice—from the punctures, tearing and
ther accidents which might occur to introduce exposure
f the flesh with resulting freezer-burn or deterioration.

Of course, you could use any can of appropriate size.
Iowever, coffee cans come with nifty snap-on plastic lids
o complete the sealing job. Moreover, a coffee can needs
nly a quick rinse before being used, whereas cans which
ontained other products would have to be thoroughly
vashed.

You probably wonder if the cans will rust. They will
ot, because all air is forced from the inside of the can
when it is filled with water, and the outside is exposed
nly to dry, cold air: in short, not a corrosive atmosphere.
And the can, of course, is plated.

I find coffee cans most useful for small pieces of fish,
ut up for frying. As to quantity, you may have to ex-
eriment a little, but generally the one-pound can holds
nough such pieces for three to five people, the two-pound
ize enough for six or eight, perhaps even ten.

Drop the pieces loosely into the can. Do not pack it
ightly, although you may shake the can to settle the pieces
nd perhaps make room for one or two more. Leave enough
oom at the top so that water can cover all the fish and

still leave a little room for expansion of the ice as it freeze
A half-inch is plenty.

Fill the can with water from the cold tap. Let it sit
few seconds until all air bubbles disappear. Then ad
more water, if necessary, to reach the desired level—abou
a half-inch below the lip.

Now all that's left is to snap on the lid and freeze. Us
a black felt marker to write the contents and the date o
freezing on the lid.

Small whole fillets and small panfish also fit well int
the cans—especially the two-pound cans. Larger fillet
often can be rolled up loosely and fitted inside. Fish steak
often stack up very neatly in the two-pound container.

Freezing Fish in Coffee Cans

1. Cut into serving-size pieces, placed in a coffee can and covere
with water, fish will freeze rapidly and maintain fresh taste fa
longer than with any other method of wrapping or containerizin
Plastic lid affords tight seal.

With a felt-tip marker, write pertinent data on top of plastic
[li]d—kind of fish, date frozen, number of servings.

Any whole fish, large steak or other configuration too
[b]ig to fit the can must, of course, be wrapped separately
[fo]r freezing.

By far the best wrapping material is heavy-duty wrapping
[p]aper, plastic-coated on one side. Light plastic wrap, plastic
[b]ags and aluminum foil are other possibilities, but not so
[go]od. Foil is well suited for the job, but punctures easily
[if] your foods get shuffled around in the freezer.

Naturally, if you intend to eat the fish within a few
[d]ays, you can use any of the airtight wraps. A puncture
[o]r two is not likely to cause freezer burn.

To wrap fish properly, tear off a piece of paper large
[e]nough to cover the length and breadth with considerable
[o]verlap. Proceed as shown in the illustrations below by
[b]ringing the sides together atop the fish and folding down
[s]everal times until snug.

After you have wrapped the ends, it's a good idea to
[s]eal them with tape to prevent loosening later.

A grease pencil can be used to mark paper or foil, so

51

long as the surface is not wet. Some felt markers wi work, even on a damp surface.

If you are freezing fish in plastic bags, it's all too eas to trap air inside when you seal the bag—which is th very thing you're trying to avoid by wrapping it up in th first place. To prevent this, hold the mouth of the ba open after putting in the fish, and dip the whole work into a sink or pail of water—taking care that no wate seeps over the mouth and inside the bag. Water pressur will force air out of the bag. Twist the bag closed jus under the surface.

Wrapping for Freezing

Whole fish, big fillets or steaks cannot be frozen in coffee can: They must be carefully wrapped, with suitable material, and kep as air-tight as possible. Heavy-duty freezer paper, plasticized on on side, is the best material. Aluminum foil is good, but can be pund tured by other frozen foods in a crowded freezer—allowing entr of air and subsequent dry spots called "freezer burn." Whateve material is chosen, wrapping procedure is the same.

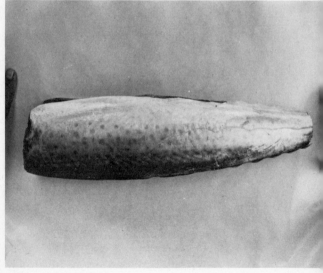

1. Use a large enough sheet of wrap to allow plenty of overlap o top and at both ends.

2. Fold the wrap several times over top of the fish.

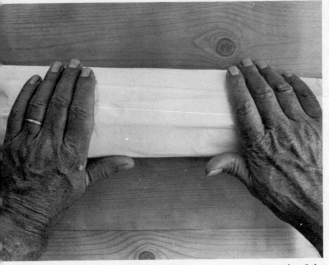

3. Continue making the folds until they are snug against the fish, then press carefully with your hands all around to force out air.

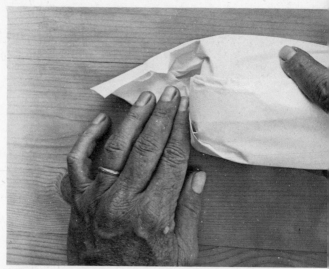

4. Fold ends—again pressing the paper tight against fish and leaving as little air space as you can.

5. Fold end wraps to underside and secure to package with freezer tape.

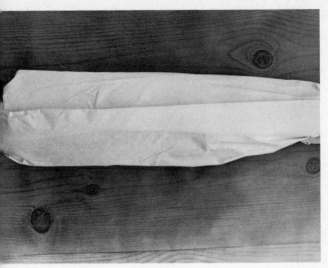

. Finished package.

THAWING FROZEN FISH

Ideally, wrapped fish should be removed from the freezer a day ahead of time and placed in the refrigerator for slow thawing. It is inadvisable to thaw fish at room temperature, but you can quick-thaw, if need be, by removing the wrap, putting the fish in a plastic bag and immersing it in a pan of cold water.

To thaw fish frozen in a coffee can, I run cold water over the outside of the can until the contents can be slipped out easily when the can is inverted. What comes out is a cylindrical chunk of ice with the fish inside it.

I hold the chunk under running cold water until all visible ice has melted. At this stage, the fish is still solid. I return it to the can, replace the lid, and stand the can upright in a sink of cold water until thawing is complete. Water need not cover the can. Usually it takes one to two hours to thaw fully.

Do not thaw fish in the can without first melting away the majority of the ice. If you did so, the fish would be

sitting for a considerable time in water—and that's
no-no, as has already been stressed.

It really isn't necessary for fish to be fully thawed if
you're going to broil, bake or boil it. Cooking time will
be increased, of course, but that's of little concern. You
could even take a foil-wrapped fish from the freezer and
put it directly into the oven for baking, but before doing
so be sure to check for punctures. After the fish has
cooked for a half hour or so, you can open the foil and
add any onion or seasonings you might wish to. Then
close the foil and go on with the cooking.

I recommend that fish for frying be thawed completely.
It's *possible* to fry partly thawed fish, but inadvisable because the temperature of the oil may drop suddenly below
the proper frying level. If the pieces are quite small, you
can get by with it by allowing a minute or two between
panfuls to let the grease get properly hot again.

SHIPPING OR TRANSPORTING FISH

Sportsmen often make long trips these days in quest of
angling opportunities different from those in their own
neighborhoods. There's no longer any good reason why
they can't get their catch home—even all the way across
the country, or from abroad.

The surest way is to bring it as personal baggage, and
the first step is to dress the fish and wrap it in freezer
paper, foil or plastic bags, and have it frozen. Many fishing camps and resorts have freezing facilities on the prem-
ises. If not, you can often arrange to have your catch
frozen at an ice house or commercial cold storage facility.

Shortly before departure time, the fish can be packed
in any kind of sturdy container, whether insulated or not.
Excellent insulation can be accomplished simply by sur-
rounding the packed fish with crumpled newspaper. Rip
the newspaper sheets apart and wad them loosely by hand.
Be sure to arrange a layer of paper on top and bottom of
the package, and on all sides.

For maximum results, the package then should be sealed
with tape. With it so packed, you can be confident the fish

will come through the airplane trip with flying colors. When you get home, chances are you'll find the fish as solid as when you started—even if eight or ten hours have elapsed.

Similar procedures can be followed if you're shipping fish, rather than having it accompany you as baggage; however, it's a good idea to provide additional insulation in case there should be an unforeseen delay in delivery.

If you can get guaranteed same-day delivery, and are certain someone will be on hand to accept the delivery at the appointed time, then the kind of packing described previously will do the job. Otherwise, try this:

Buy one of the inexpensive plastic-foam coolers large enough to hold all your frozen fish. Put the fish inside it, and fill all remaining space with crumpled newspaper. Position the lid tightly and carefully seal all the edges with tape. Run additional strips of tape, for support, around the entire box.

Since such a cooler is flimsy and may not withstand much rough handling, it should be then placed inside a large cardboard box. If the fit between the two boxes isn't snug, once more you use crumpled newspaper for padding.

The resulting package will keep fish frozen for a good three days. Once I took delivery of fish which were so packed, after they had gone astray and been delayed a full five days. They still were satisfactorily frozen, with only a bit of thawing around the edges.

When you get your fish home, transfer them directly to the home freezer if they were wrapped properly at the distant location. But if you think a more satisfactory wrapping job can be done at home—for instance, transferring the fish to coffee cans or re-wrapping with heavier freezer paper—by all means do so.

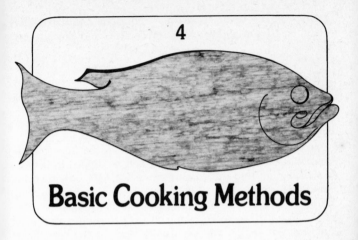

4

Basic Cooking Methods

Many times I've heard the lament, "I just can't cook fish." Maybe you've heard it yourself. Maybe you've *said* it yourself. If so, don't give up yet. Chances are you can pin your failure on just one simple error: over-cooking.

Unlike other meats, which often become more tender with longer cooking, fish just gets drier, and usually tougher. Serve up your fish while it's still flaky and juicy and you'll get compliments, not complaints.

No matter whether you're serving plain fried fish or one of the more elaborate fish recipes with numerous other ingredients, it's important to master the basic cooking methods, and always with the cardinal rule in mind— *don't over-cook.*

Fish belongs on the menu regularly. Most of the time it should be prepared by one of the basic methods—frying, broiling, baking or steaming. The delicate fresh-fish flavor, which we have so devoutly strived to maintain in preceding chapters, is thus brought forth in full blossom.

FRYING

Fried fish is the favorite of most folks, calories and cholesterol notwithstanding. It should be brown and crisp on the outside, flaky and moist on the inside. And never greasy. All of which is easier said than done, but not really too hard if a few simple procedures and precautions are followed.

First, there's the coating.

If you are frying fish which have been scaled but not skinned—panfish or fillets with the skin left on—the fish should be moistened lightly with water or milk, and dipped in either flour or corn meal or a half-and-half mixture of both.

Because there is no skin to help hold in the juices, skinless fillets or pieces of fish should first be dipped in beaten egg, and then into the coating of choice. My own favorite coatings for this are corn flake crumbs and packaged bread crumbs. Cracker meal, corn meal or flour may also be used. You'll have to try them all to determine your own favorite, but I'll bet you eventually vote for the corn flake crumbs.

Another option is to use a batter instead of egg-and-crumbs. I normally use the corn flakes, but I like the batter well enough to switch from time to time. To make the batter, mix the following ingredients, then beat them to the consistency of heavy cream:

2 eggs
½ tsp. sugar
4 heaping tbsp. flour
milk to obtain creamy consistency

Dip the pieces of fish (dry) in the batter.

Batter makes the job easy in that you can put the fish and batter in a large bowl, mix thoroughly to coat the fish, and then fork the pieces out of the bowl and directly into the frying pan.

The best way to operate the mechanics of the egg-and-crumb method is to start by beating two eggs in a bowl large enough to hold all the fish. Put the fish in the bowl and mix thoroughly to coat the pieces well. With your crumbs in a heavy paper bag, fork the egg-coated pieces of fish into the bag, there or four at a time. Shake the bag, supporting the bottom of it with one hand. Remove the pieces and place them on a platter or sheet of waxed paper. Continue until all pieces are coated, and then proceed with the frying.

In the actual frying, time and temperature are the keys. And if you get the temperature right, the timing will take care of itself.

You not only must get the right temperature, but you must *keep it*. Because of this, fish should be fried in either a cast-iron skillet or one of heavy-gauge aluminum. Thin aluminum pans get too hot, too fast, and then lose heat rapidly when fish are loaded.

The best temperature is in the range of 375 to 400 degrees. An electric frying pan with thermostat can be very helpful. When cooking on a range, you should find the medium-high setting about right, and with a little trial-and-error experience you should be able to maintain the proper temperature, even without a thermometer.

If I have any doubts, I test-fry one piece of fish. It should sizzle vigorously as soon as it hits the oil, and brown on one side in not much more than a minute. I like to turn the fish once and brown the other side equally for, at the most, another minute.

As to oil, I prefer vegetable oil or vegetable shortening. Peanut oil is my favorite. Animal fat covers up the fish flavor.

In my view, the pieces of fish should not be more than an inch thick, and there should be ample oil in the pan to cover. Don't skimp on the oil. It can be strained afterward and used again.

My frying implement is a long-handled slotted spoon. Remove the pieces one or two at a dip (if the spoon will hold more than one) and hold over the pan until oil has stopped dripping through the slots in the spoon. Then drop the pieces on absorbent paper.

Stay with it until all the fish is cooked. Don't be pulled away by the phone or doorbell. As soon as the pan is empty, fill it up again, and continue until the job is done.

You'll notice I haven't mentioned salt and pepper. I

sprinkle both over the individual pieces of fish before I dip or coat them. I've tried to take a shortcut by adding salt to the crumbs in the bag, but I never seem to hit it right.

Hush Puppies

Hush puppies go with fried fish like pretzels with beer. They can be prepared beforehand and fried immediately after the fish—at the same temperature and in jig time.

From a meager beginning of corn meal, salt and water, hush puppies have blossomed through the years into many glamorous forms, varied by such additional ingredients as flour, eggs, sugar, shortening, onions, beer, molasses, tomato juice and wine. So adaptable, and so nearly foolproof, is this fried bread that virtually everybody who makes hush puppies regularly has some special ingredient or combination which constitutes "his own special recipe."

If you haven't tried hush puppies before, try this simple style to start. It's the one I still use most of the time, although I do elaborate now and then.

1 cup self-rising corn meal
1 small onion, grated
leftover egg from breading fish (if any)
about one-third cup milk

Put the meal in a small bowl and grate the onion directly into it. Add the egg, and then the milk, slowly—stirring until the batter is moist, yet stiff enough to hold shape when formed or when dropped from a spoon. I prefer to form each hush puppy into the shape of a tiny football and drop it into the hot oil by hand. It's faster, however, simply to dip by the half-tablespoon directly into the pan.

Fry at fish-frying temperature, turning once to brown on each side.

Self-rising corn meal is a marvelous convenience. Without it, you would have to mix a bit of flour, baking powder and salt into regular meal. Self-rising meal is a stock item throughout the South and in some other sections of the country, but not available everywhere.

62

As already hinted, it's possible to stray from the basic hush puppy recipe in any number of directions, and I often do. For instance:

1. Chop the onion instead of grating. Or leave the onion out, if you must.

2. Substitute tomato juice, beer or wine for the milk.

3. If you like sweet hush puppies (I don't, particularly), add a couple teaspoons of molasses, sugar or syrup.

The only thing you really have to guard against in experimenting with your own special hush puppy mixture is getting the batter too soupy. If you use egg, grated onion, molasses or other liquidy ingredients, then you naturally have to cut down on the amount of your primary liquid (beer, milk or whatever).

Here is my favorite of all hush puppy recipes—the amount doubled because I usually make it only for company occasions:

2 cups self-rising meal

1 large onion, grated

1 beaten egg (definitely, whether leftover from fish or not)

1 can of fish roe (from the grocer; most large stores carry this)

Tomato juice or V-8 juice for desired consistency

This recipe will serve seven or eight.

BROILED FISH

It's a snap to turn out delicious broiled fish, but again you should stay close to the scene of action and guard against over-cooking. For broiling, choose either fillets or steaks up to an inch thick. These can be broiled without turning. If your steaks are much thicker than an inch, they must be turned, but this is no great problem.

Place the broiler rack about four or five inches (no more) under the heat unit. Allow the unit to pre-heat for just a few minutes.

Cover a cookie sheet or shallow broiling pan with aluminum foil, turning up the edges all around to minimize cleanup chores later.

Arrange fish on the foil, skin side down if there is a skin side. Sprinkle with salt and black pepper. Place pan under the broiler just long enough to make the surface of the fish fairly hot. Remove the pan and coat all fish generously with butter or margarine. Because the fish is hot, you can spear a large pat of butter with a fork and slide this over each fillet. It's faster, easier, and just as efficient as melting butter and applying it with a brush.

Now return the pan to the oven, leaving the oven door ajar. Allow the fish to broil for ten minutes, then remove and check for doneness by sticking a fork gently into the thickest portion. The meat should flake easily all the way through. If so, it's ready. If not, apply another coating of butter and return it to the oven for another three minutes or so.

If you are broiling a steak more than an inch thick, turn it at the end of the ten minutes, brush with butter, and cook for three or four more minutes.

In broiling, the fatty fish, such as mackerel and bluefish, need be treated no differently from the lean ones, such as snapper. However, you should perhaps apply the butter more liberally to those varieties which have little fat of their own. And if your diet nixes the use of butter or margarine, choose the fatty kinds, since they broil well enough without it, although much better with it.

SAUTÉING

With this type of cooking you use a frying pan with just a little butter, margarine or oil. It is also called "pan broiling" if the fish is cooked without any sort of coating, or "pan frying" if flour is used.

Somewhat lower temperatures are used than in normal or deep frying, the ideal being about 325 degrees, or medium. Otherwise the surface might brown much too fast, and begin to scorch or burn before the fish is completely cooked. This is especially true when using butter or margarine.

Sautéing can be chosen either for fillets or for small whole fish, such as bluegill or stream trout. If you care about eye-appeal, dust the moistened fish with flour. Un-

loured fillets tend to come apart more easily, and un-
loured whole fish will end up with numerous breaks in the
skin. But if you're going to eat the fish and not take pic-
ures of them, it doesn't matter a bit. And I prefer to leave
ff the flour, not only because I like the taste of the simple,
an-broiled fish, but also because flouring makes the tem-
erature business even more tricky. Over-browning is too
asy with flour.

Sautéed fish should be turned only once, as soon as the
rst side is browned. And here I should point out that
browned" is a relative term. Without coating, fish does not
eally take on the overall golden hue provided by batter or
crumbs. It should be turned when the edges take on a crisp
rownish tone while most of the center portion is an appetiz-
ng yellowish-tan.

After turning and cooking for another minute or two,
est for doneness with a fork, piercing gently to make sure
he meat flakes through (or flakes to the bone in the case of
whole fish).

After your fish is sautéed, you can add a little lemon juice,
crape the pan with a spatula, and thus make a simple but
elicious sauce for pouring over the fish.

BAKING

A whole baked fish, either with or without the head, is
ne of the most attractive dishes you can put on the table—
nd it tastes even better than it looks. Some people just
on't like the idea of a fish head on their platter, but there
s a practical side as well as a visual one. The head of a
sh contains a surprising amount of meat—mostly around
he "cheeks" and the top of the head. And in most species,
he head meat is even more tasty, and lighter-textured, than
he fillet meat. A lot of folks consider it a special treat.

At any rate, choose a fish weighing between two and
ight pounds. You can, of course, bake fish weighing a
ound or less, but will have to allot at least one fish per
erson.

Cover a shallow baking pan with aluminum foil, and on
his lay the fish, which has been patted dry with a paper

65

towel. The fish can be stuffed or not, as you like. Make sure the oven has been pre-heated to 350 degrees, and then put the pan on a shelf in the center of the oven.

Although the skin helps retain the juices, you should still do a little basting. As prescribed for broiled fish, you can let the fish heat for a few minutes, and then rub the surface with a pat of butter or margarine. After about fifteen or twenty minutes, rub again with butter.

Or you might use bacon. Before putting your fish in the oven, lay two or three strips of bacon across the top. No further basting will be needed, and the skin protects the fish from absorbing more than just a delicate hint of the bacon flavor.

Cooking time will vary from as little as thirty minutes for a two-pound fish to as much as an hour and a half for an eight-pounder. Again, you should rely on testing more than timing, and avoid cooking too long.

With a two- or three-pound fish, test with a fork after thirty or forty minutes. At the thickest portion, just back of the head, the meat should flake to the bone and not show any pink. If the fish weighs five pounds you can safely put off the test until after one hour of cooking.

One reason that testing is important is that thermostats on many older ovens may not be accurate. Whether the fish is put in cold or at room temperature can make a difference too.

Fish weighing less than two pounds will normally bake to perfection in twenty to thirty minutes. Otherwise, they should be treated exactly as for larger ones—basting either with butter or bacon strips.

Fillets and steaks can be baked too, but they should either be basted very liberally, or wrapped in aluminum foil to prevent drying. Baking temperature remains 350 degrees. Cooking time probably will be fifteen to thirty minutes, depending on the size of the pieces.

POACHING, STEAMING OR BOILING

All three of those terms may be used to describe the same basic cooking procedure, but the word "boiling" as applied to fish raises my hackles a bit. To me, boiling means bubbling around in a lot of water, and with fish this is a real no-no—except when making a fast chowder.

Salmon (and also large trout) are delicious when steaked and poached. So are all the members of the saltwater tuna family. The lean, white-meat fishes of both fresh and salt water are seldom poached, but are not bad at all when prepared this way—especially when served in a salad with some oil or mayonnaise.

Boil barely enough lightly-salted water to cover steaks or chunks about one and a half to two inches thick. Add two tablespoons of vegetable oil or margarine to the water. Add fish, cover, and reduce heat to simmer. Simmer for eight or ten minutes, or until fish flakes with a fork. Drain immediately. Most poached fish is served cold.

A common variation is to poach the fish in court bouillon rather than water. Court bouillon is a light broth made by boiling carrots, celery, onion and spices, along with fish stock. The recipe is given in Chapter 6.

And when you start going over the "fancy" fish recipes in Chapter 6 and outside sources, you'll notice that most of them are simply the basic fish-cooking methods we have just outlined—with additions and embellishments, mainly in sauces or additives.

A thorough familiarity with the basic cooking procedures will help assure that any gourmet touches you wish to add through specific recipes turn out the way they're supposed to.

5

Cooking Fish Outdoors

Does fish really taste better when you cook it outdoors? Of course it does—but not because any new or different flavors are obtained from the fish itself. Taste, after all (and this is a scientific fact), is far more than the simple result of brushing food against taste buds. Many other elements contribute to it—aroma, texture, color, setting and psychological mood.

Probably you've met people who claim they "don't like fish," yet at a streamside cookout will even snitch your share if you look away for a moment.

Considering the universal enthusiasm for out-of-doors fish cookery, it's strange indeed that so many backyard chefs never give a thought to preparing fish on the home grill. Perhaps they have finally mastered the perfect charcoal steak or hamburger, and are unwilling to risk their reputations by trying something new.

It could be, though, that they've tried to grill fish, only to end up with a tough and tasteless product, or have seen fillets flake away before their eyes and disappear through the grill onto the coals.

Grilling fish can indeed be tricky if your barbecuing experience has been limited to red meat. Still, it certainly isn't difficult. The first thing to remember is that ample and frequent basting with butter or a prepared basting sauce is an absolute necessity, even with fatty fish such as salmon and kingfish.

Also, you will find it rather difficult to cook the fish directly on the grill. It can be done, but unless you take great pains in turning, your fish is apt to flake into pieces. Liberal oiling of the grill is helpful, but not infallible.

Some types and cuts of fish handle much better than others when laid on the grill. Fish steaks, for example, are sort of bound by the circling strip of skin. Whole fish, with skin intact, will obviously be more cooperative than a skinless fillet.

The easy way to solve all such problems, however, is to buy yourself a wire-frame broiler with handle. These are available wherever barbecuing equipment is sold. The fish is held firmly between two wire sides, and can be turned easily. You can baste right through the frame, and there is an added advantage in that *all* your pieces of fish get turned over in one quick motion.

Before putting a fish into the broiler, it should be rubbed with vegetable oil on both sides. Oil the broiler as well, and for further protection against sticking, you can place strips of bacon between the fish and the wire.

Even if the fish does stick, no tragedy results. You might not be able to put a neat and pretty product on your guests' plates, but when they taste it, they won't mind.

Your grill should be a good four inches above the coals, or six inches for thick steaks or whole small fish. Place the wire broiler on the grill. Turn and baste the fish after a couple of minutes, using melted butter with lemon juice, or a favorite marinade that contains oil. Average-size fillets and small whole fish will require five to ten minutes of cooking on each side. Large ones will take more time, of course. As with all grill cooking, the chef must be observant and ever ready to raise or lower the grill as required by variation in the heat being put forth by the coals. Should the first get too hot—and the grill at its highest point—it may be necessary to sprinkle water on the coals.

You should aim for an attractive browned finish on the outside, with the inside moist and flaky. After a couple of efforts, you'll probably be able to let your eyes be your guide, but until you have built such confidence, test the fish often for doneness. If a fork slides easily all the way through the flesh (to the spine in the case of a whole fish), it's ready. Should you want a double check, use the fork to flake away a bit of meat down to the centermost portion.

Basting should be done at least twice on each side, several times if cooking exceeds ten minutes.

Another fine way to cook fish on your backyard grill is to wrap individual servings in aluminum foil, place the packages on the grill, and turn with tongs from time to time until done—usually twenty to thirty minutes. While you could get exactly the same results in your kitchen oven, your guests will still be delighted because it's served outdoors.

Aluminum-foil cookery is always the same, whatever the setting or the heat source. For more details, see the section on Campfire Cooking later in this chapter.

GRILL-SMOKING

If you own a covered grill you can produce fish dishes that will make you the rave of the neighborhood. By means of a system called grill-smoking or hot-smoking, your fish will emerge with a marvelous smoke taste, and with much less time and effort than is required for true smoked fish.

Besides the covered grill, you'll need only two important items—a brine solution made by dissolving a cup of salt in three quarts of cold water, and some hickory sawdust or chips. A pound of the chips should be soaked in a half-gallon of water for about a half hour before using.

A low temperature is required for this style of smoke-cooking, the ideal being somewhere in the range of 150 to 300 degrees. With electric or gas grills you have only to set the thermostat. With a charcoal grill, use fewer briquettes than you would for ordinary grilling, and spread them out more thinly in the pan.

Marinate your fish in brine solution for approximately forty-five minutes. After your coals are glowing and well spread out, cover them with a heavy handful of the wet sawdust, making sure that every coal is covered.

71

Now remove fish from the brine and pat dry with a paper towel. Brush with vegetable oil, margarine or butter. Place them on the grill or, better yet, use the wire-frame broiler mentioned previously. Close the cover.

The wet sawdust produces plenty of smoke and also helps keep the temperature at the desired low level.

Raise the cover every ten to fifteen minutes to baste the fish liberally and to check the sawdust supply. Add more wet dust as needed. And don't skimp on it.

Cooking time may vary from as little as thirty minutes to, occasionally, a couple of hours—depending not only on the cut of the fish, but on the temperature of your particular cooker, and variations in temperature caused by the frequent opening or by outside weather influences.

Use the aforementioned checks for doneness. And if your fish seems to be taking extraordinarily long to cook, don't worry about it at all. Nothing can go wrong. You'll just have time to serve another beer or two.

The hot-smoking technique can also be used with a stuffed fish, or with a stuffed double fillet. Marinate the fish first, as described, then fill with the selected dressing and secure the whole shebang in a wire broiler. Then proceed the same way—basting and replacing the sawdust often. Average cooking time for this is about an hour and a half.

SMOKING FISH

Though it may taste much the same, true smoked fish is derived from an entirely different process from grill-smoking. It must be done in a smoking chamber which is made according to rigid requirements of heat and circulation. Of course, smoking is a preservation process. Fish or other meat so treated will last far longer than fresh meats. You can keep smoked fish in your refrigerator (wrapped or covered) for weeks on end. In a freezer, it will last indefinitely.

A workable smoker can be home-made, out of such containers as an old refrigerator, or a metal ice chest, or a discarded wall oven. All you have to do is arrange wire racks inside, provide for entrance of air at the bottom of the unit plus a small exit hole at the top, and come up with some source of very low heat. An electric hot plate is often used.

But all that is still a lot of trouble—especially since commercially-manufactured smokers are available at very low cost. They work beautifully, stow without trouble in the average household, and need only be plugged in to start working. And one filling will produce enough smoked fish to last a big family a long time.

You may not be aware of it, but the smoke does not contribute anything to the actual curing of the fish. It only adds flavor. Curing is accomplished by slowly drawing moisture from the flesh.

You begin the moisture-withdrawing process by soaking the fish for quite a long time in a heavy brine solution, after which you remove it from the brine and allow it to air-dry and take on a glaze. Then it is placed in the smoker, on wire racks, and cured for at least several more hours, surrounded within the smoker by smoke and low heat— usually in the neighborhood of 100 to 180 degrees. The heat slowly draws remaining moisture from the fish, and at the same time allows the smoky flavor to penetrate.

Smoking fish at home is a time-consuming process but certainly a simple one. The smoker can be used outside, on a patio or walkway, or in a carport. Or it can be used inside in a fireplace—which is advisable if the outside temperature falls below 70 degrees.

For brine-curing, dissolve one cup of curing salt, one cup of rock salt and two cups of sugar in a quart of water. Mix additional amounts in the same proportions if you need more to cover the amount of fish you have.

Fillets make for more satisfactory smoked fish than do steaks, though the latter can be used. Leave the skin on and cut the fillets into pieces small enough to be easily arranged on the racks of your smoker.

Submerge the fish in the brine solution, using a glass, plastic or earthenware bowl as a container. Do not use metal, since all metals are affected by salt.

Place some sort of weight atop the fish (a dinner plate usually does it) so that no ends stick above the surface.

Leave submerged for six hours.

At the end of the brining time, rinse the fish, piece by piece, under cold running water, and lay on paper toweling. Pat all surfaces dry with more towels, and let the fish dry at room temperature for about an hour, or until a noticeable glaze forms on the surface.

As soon as you begin the air-drying period, plug in your smoker for it to pre-heat.

The racks of my smoker can be removed in one unit for convenience and portability. When the brined fish takes on its glaze, you arrange the pieces on the racks so they are not touching. Place thicker pieces on the lower racks, since that will be the hottest area during smoking time.

The smoking will take approximately six hours. Smoke is provided by filling a small pan with prepared hickory sawdust and placing it atop the heating unit in the bottom of the smoker. A full pan will burn out in something less than an hour. The manufacturer recommends refilling the pan four times during a six-hour spell of smoking—or about every one and a half hours. But since the smoke has nothing to do with the actual cooking-curing process, you could fill the pan less often or more often, with resulting variations in the amount of "smoky taste." I agree that four pans is about right.

You should begin checking for doneness after four hours. Some of the thin pieces might be ready that soon. It so, the outside will have a dark, rich look to it. But to be doubly sure, take out a piece and break it. The meat should flake easily in the middle.

As you try different species in your smoker, you'll develop your own preferences, but don't be afraid to try any of your favorite kinds. Everything doesn't have to be smoked salmon, or smoked sturgeon, or smoked sailfish. Smoked fillets of largemouth bass and many other "everyday" fish of fresh and salt water are scrumptious.

I prefer my smoked fish done as simply as possible—just as explained. Some like exotic spices and flavorings, such as onion or garlic, ginger or nutmeg. If you wish to try any or all of these, add them to the brine solution, or rub them into the meat after brining but before smoking.

If you buy one of the commercial home smokers, you'll get detailed instructions not only for fish but for meats and other foods as well.

CAMP STOVE COOKING

A fisherman need not be a camper to enjoy the benefits of a small portable stove. The two-burner models, fueled by LP gas cylinders or by liquid gasoline, can do an outstanding job of frying fish—whether on an overnight campout, an all-day float trip or simply a picnic. For back-packing, or stowing in limited space, you can find a number of small, one-burner units that operate on a variety of fuels. These too can fry fish satisfactorily, provided you use a small pan and don't attempt to cook too many pieces at a time.

One of my own pet uses for a one-burner LP foldable stove is to cook fresh-caught fish for my lunch while I'm out fishing. I cook them right in the skiff if for some reason I don't wish to go ashore.

After all, why should an angler eat a bologna sandwich for his lunch when he can just as easily feast on the very delicacy he's out there to get in the first place?

No great amount of equipment or extra luggage is involved. I carry everything needed in a canvas bag fourteen inches long by ten inches wide by ten inches high—kitchen, pantry, the whole works. Everything but the fish, which is left to angling skill and diligence. Not that I don't have faith in my ability to dredge up enough fish for lunch, but I keep a can of corned beef in that bag too. Just in case the frying pan falls overboard or something.

The "shore dinner" is a long-established custom at camps throughout the country and in Canada. The guide carries along the fixings, and when lunch time rolls around, he pulls the boat to shore and cooks the fish while his anglers catch a snooze in the shade.

That's the best approach of all, but without a guide you do it yourself. You can rip through the whole operation in a half hour or less, and maybe still have time for that nap before the next tide, or while waiting for the sun to get just a little lower.

If you can find the right spot on shore, you'll probably

enjoy the whole thing a little more, because you can get out of the boat, and find a nice shady spot and enjoy the stretch and the elbow room. But sometimes the convenient shorelines are too wet, or too thick, or harbor a band of mosquitoes who are looking for a good meal themselves.

In that case, anchor the boat and cook away right there.

Here is a list of supplies I carry in the aforementioned small bag:

Equipment

1-burner butane stove	Plastic forks and spoons
7-inch cast-iron skillet	Paper cups (for hot drinks)
Slotted spoon	Small pot for boiling water
2 small plastic bowls	Paper towels and plates

Supplies

Small can shortening	Instant coffee
Corn flake crumbs	Instant chocolate
Self-rising corn meal	Instant soups
Dehydrated onion	Tea bags
Salt and pepper	Sugar packets
	Dry coffee creamer

It takes almost as much room to list that stuff as to carry it. But none are exceptionally bulky except the stove and the frying pan. Salt, pepper and onion are in shaker-size tubes, which can be tucked inside larger items. The drinks and soup are in small envelopes for individual servings.

A nice by-product of carrying such a kit is that within a couple of minutes you can have a hot drink or cup of soup.

The only think you *really* need that can't be carried in the kit is a jug of water. Perishables are entirely optional, but can be carried in your ice chest—such things as tomatoes, salad in a plastic bag, or fruit.

I generally carry an egg in the ice chest (inside a small jar) because my favorite coating for skinless fish fillets is beaten egg and corn flake crumbs (see Chapter 4). But

76

when I cook panfish, I just moisten them and shake with corn meal.

At lunch time, I set up the stove and light it and put on the pan with grease so it can heat while other preparations are being made. There is almost no chance of the grease getting too hot on the small stove in open air. In fact, it might not get hot enough if you try to use a thin aluminum skillet instead of cast iron.

While the grease is heating, I clean and fillet the fish, or scale and draw panfish, and sprinkle it with salt and pepper. I beat the egg in one of the plastic bowls if fillets are the course of the day, add the cut-up fillets to the egg, and toss to coat them thoroughly. Then I drop the pieces, two or three at a time, into a paper bag. After a good shake, they are removed to a paper towel.

In the other bowl, I put a teaspoon of dried onion and a little water—letting this sit while I finish mealing the fish. When the onion has sat about five minutes, I add about a cup of self-rising meal and extra water or other handy liquid, if necessary, to make a moist but stiff batter (see hush puppy recipe in Chapter 4).

Now I'm ready to get rolling. If a drop of water makes a loud sizzle in the pan, I start frying the fish by depositing from two to four pieces at a time in the grease. I never crowd too many pieces in the pan, as I must make sure the temperature doesn't fall very much.

I turn the fish once, and as each piece gets golden brown, I remove it with the slotted spoon and deposit it on paper towels.

Once all the fish is cooked, I dip thumb-sized bits of the hush puppy batter into the pan, which will easily accommodate about eight or ten puppies at one time. These must be turned once to brown on both sides, and they cook considerably faster than the fish.

When everything is fried, I remove the pan to a safe place to cool, protecting the deck of the boat with paper plates or anything handy that can serve as a hot pad.

I put on a pot of water immediately, and in a few more minutes everyone aboard can have his choice of hot drinks.

After lunch the pan should be cool enough so that I can pour the grease back into its can, wipe the skillet with paper towels, and start putting everything back into the canvas bag. The only other dirty dishes are two bowls and a spoon, which can be rinsed overside and wiped.

There will be a lot of litter, though—plates, cups, plastic forks and copious paper towels. I pack these in a paper or plastic bag and stow for disposal when I get back to shore.

Roughly the same procedures, and the same check-list of supplies, can be used when you're cooking larger quantities of fish on a two-burner stove for more people—perhaps at a picnic, or maybe at streamside for a mealtime rendezvous with other boats. Quantities may have to be increased, and larger utensils used.

PLANNING A FISH-FRY

Maybe there isn't an easy way to stage a cookout for a large number of people. But at least there's a fairly inexpensive way, if you're a fisherman who manages to stockpile enough fish.

With proper planning, little enough trouble is involved— especially if you can stick your wife (or some of the guests) with taking care of table settings and complementary food items such as beans, salad and cold drinks.

Figure the amount of fish required as follows:

> Fillets—one quarter pound per person
> Steaks—one half pound per person
> Panfish—one pound per person

Add a couple of pounds "for the pot" if you wish to play it safe, but those figures are surprisingly accurate, and when a rather large and diverse crowd is involved there almost always will be leftovers.

Make most of your preparations at home. Cut the fish into serving-size pieces and salt it. Then pack it in a covered plastic container or a plastic bag for temporary holding in a portable cooler.

Hush puppies also should be mixed in advance and stored in a Tupperware container or a covered bowl. The hush puppy recipe given in Chapter 4 will serve five. Make it in necessary multiples, figuring one egg for each two cups of self-rising corn meal.

Your challenge is to turn out quantities of fish, fast enough for all the guests to enjoy it piping hot. To do this, you must bring your grease to the appropriate high temperature, keep it there throughout the cooking, and set up an efficient operating system.

As soon as you arrive at the site, fire up the stove. A two-burner camp stove can be depended upon to do the job, and to utilize it to best advantage you should consider a large, rectangular skillet of cast iron. These are not easily found on housewares counters, but you might get one through a restaurant supply house, or perhaps a metal shop can turn one out for you at reasonable cost.

If you do decide to have one made, specify dimensions which fit neatly over *both* burners of your stove. For deep-frying fish on small burners, two fires are better than one.

Without such a special cooker, you must use the largest skillet your main burner will accommodate. The second burner on most camp stoves is an auxiliary and doesn't attain the heat possible with the main one. But you can use a smaller skillet there, and by allowing extra heating time, make helpful use of it.

While the grease heats in your pan (or pans), bread the fish. Beat two or three eggs in a large bowl, fill the bowl with pieces of ready-salted fish, and toss thoroughly. With a fork, bread the pieces by shaking them in a bag with corn flake crumbs, and remove them to a tray or cookie sheet.

Continue until all the fish is breaded. If flies are around, cover the fish with strips of paper towel. Put more paper toweling into one or more large baking pans, or other suitable receptacles, for the fish after it is cooked.

Test-fry one piece of fish to determine if the grease is ready. If you're using two skillets, test a piece in each of them. If the fish browns nicely within two minutes or so, you should be in good shape to start the production line.

Lay out your tray of fish, the hush puppy mix and the take-up pans within easy reach. From now until everything that's uncooked disappears, focus your complete attention on the task at hand.

Drop pieces of fish gently into the pans, until a comfortable capacity is reached. Within a minute, the earliest pieces should be starting to brown. Remove these with a slotted spoon and add others.

Very shortly, you should reach the point where you are constantly dipping up some of the pieces and replacing them. From time to time, hold up on new fish and, instead, drop six or eight hush puppies into the pan with a tablespoon.

At home, I cook all the fish and then all the hush puppies. On a fish-fry, however, I cook ample quantities of both at one time—so that the chow line can begin forming right away.

Rinse your hush puppy spoon in a cup of water now and then. It will make dipping and dropping much easier.

Sooner than you think, the whole job is done. Turn off the burners, join the rest of the picnickers, and enjoy both the hot fish and the compliments you're bound to receive.

CAMPFIRE COOKING

Cooking at an open fire with pots and pans, or wire racks and grills, is not so different from cooking on a camp stove or backyard barbecue. Your main concern will be in creating and maintaining the proper amount of fire or glowing coals to do what you want.

But I do wish to talk about three proven ways to turn out tasty fish with no untensils at all—even though one of these methods requires aluminum foil.

Maybe you'll use one of these recipes someday on a hiking trip, or in an emergency. Or you might decide to build a fire on the spur of the moment when you're out fishing to cook up a little private feast.

Let's start with planked fish, which in some epicurean circles is an elaborate and involved undertaking prepared in the finest kitchens. But in this case, it simply means putting a slab of fish on a plank and propping the plank close to the fire until your meal is done.

All you need is a fish and a flat, or fairly flat, chunk of wood. Dress the fish in double-fillet style (see Chapter 2), and affix the fillet, skin side down, on the plank. The fish must be firmly pinned to the wood, in some manner, all around the edges.

A simple method is to use tacks and a hammer. But if these are not available (and they seldom are, since planking is often a spur-of-the-moment decision), cast around for a substitute.

You could use fish hooks as makeshift tacks. You could wire the fish to the board with stainless leader wire. Failing those, or any other metallic substitute, you could fashion some small wooden pins with your pocket knife, and gouge tiny holes with your knife-point to help seat the pins in the plank.

Getting the fish fastened to the plank is the only hard part. Now you prop the plank upright near your fire. It doesn't much matter whether you have a roaring blaze or a bed of hot coals. Just adjust the distance accordingly, and sit back and relax for a while.

In perhaps ten or fifteen minutes your dinner will be ready. The outside will harden and brown. Test the inside by poking it for flakiness with a pointed stick.

Pull the plank away from the fire and use it for both table and plate. If you have no tableware at all, let the fish cool a little and eat it with your fingers.

The first time I tried planked fish was out of dire necessity, when I camped out overnight involuntarily due to engine failure. I ate, expecting sustenance only—most especially because I had no salt. But, lo and behold, I not only staved off hunger but enjoyed a most delicious repast. However, I do add salt, as well as a bit of butter and lemon, when such luxuries are at hand.

A similar procedure makes use of a flat rock, and is even easier than planking, since the fish doesn't have to be nailed down. Find a rock large enough to accommodate the number of fillets you want to cook. Put the rock smack in the middle of your fire and heat it until it's sizzling hot. Rake it out of the fire with a stick and lay your fish on top of it, skin side down. Don't mind the ashes. They won't get to the meat through the skin.

This system works best with very thin fillets, up to a quarter-inch thick, and they will cook in fifteen minutes or so. When the meat flakes easily away from the skin, dig in.

Cooking with aluminum foil is not necessarily an improvement over the plank and the rock, but it demonstrates progress at work. A lot of anglers, hikers and campers keep some lengths of aluminum foil in their packs or kits—torn from the original roll and folded for tucking away.

A good bed of glowing coals is needed for foil-baking, so start your fire well in advance. Take your choice of either a small fish, around a pound, say, or a couple of fillets.

Place the fish in the center of a piece of foil large enough to allow a good wrap over the top and at both ends. The method of making the wrap is the same as the one illustrated in Chapter 3 for freezer wrapping.

However, before wrapping up the dinner package, sprinkle the fish with salt and pepper, and put in either a piece of bacon or a dab of butter, along with a liberal sprinkling of lemon juice.

Now wrap all securely and place it directly on the bed of coals. You might rake some coals over the top of the package to hasten cooking, or turn the package frequently with a stick.

If the coals stay glowing hot, twenty minutes should be ample cooking time. Carefully rake the package out of the fire to avoid puncturing the foil. Open it and give the test for doneness. If the meat should still be pink and tough in the middle, refold the package and return it to the fire.

By taking care to handle only the wraps (don't touch the parts that are directly touching the contents), you can handle foil with your fingers almost immediately without risking a bad burn. But don't go blundering to the task. Proceed delicately and use the tips of your fingers only.

If you wish, you can cook an entire meal in one of these foil packages simply by adding some slices of onion, potato and carrots to the fish. Slice all of them quite thin so they will cook as quickly as the fish.

How to Eat Panfish (Without Eating Bones)

Many people shun panfish because of the problem of eating around the bones. Here's a simple way to do it. You have to use your fingers, but etiquette be hanged at a fish fry!

1. Grasp dorsal fin near the tail end and pull gently, upward and outward—moving your grip farther forward if necessary to be sure the bones that anchor the fins all come out. Discard the whole piece you remove.

2. Remove the anal (lower) fin in the same manner.

3. Now, by biting along the backbone, you'll get all the delicious
meat. Avoid the rib-cage area, which is shown intact in the picture,
and you'll have no trouble at all with bones. Note, however, that
the meat in the rib cage is delicious, and a lot of people go to the
trouble of picking it away from the bones.

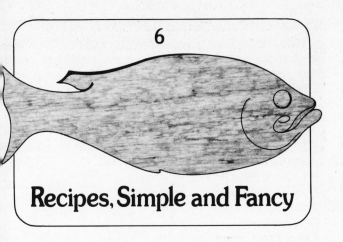

6

Recipes, Simple and Fancy

All good cooks have long since discovered that a recipe is no sacred cow which must be held inviolate down to the last pinch of salt and the last flick of a stirring spoon. With fish dishes, you have extra leeway. You can confidently add an ingredient, omit one, or vary quantities. Naturally, you shouldn't dump in two teaspoons of salt for a recipe prescribing a half-teaspoon, but if you prefer a faint hint of onion to a strong jolt, for example, act accordingly.

Familiarize yourself with the basic cooking methods covered in Chapter 4. Fish "recipes," for the most part, are simply embellishments on the basic methods.

Also, virtually all fish recipes you find in cook books or columns specify a particular species of fish. Again, substitutions are unlimited. A recipe built around a baked red snapper will work just as well for a striped bass or a husky walleye or many other kinds. The guide list in Chapter 7 makes note of the cooking methods suitable for the different species.

Some of the selected recipes which follow do name a specific fish—out of habit or tradition—but most have been generalized.

APPETIZERS

Fish—other than processed types such as anchovies, smoked fish bits and sardines—are not often seen on the hors d'oeuvres table. Here are a few home preparations which will tastily remedy that oversight.

Seviche

1 pound white-meat fish fillets, skinned and cut into bite-size strips or pieces
1 large onion, chopped or sliced
1 small green pepper, chopped fine
2 chili peppers, chopped fine
Tabasco sauce—a few drops
4 to 6 limes or lemons

This is a Latin American favorite, great as an appetizer, a first-course cocktail, or as a snack with cold beer. Is it raw fish? Not at all. Marinading in lime juice cooks it as thoroughly as any fire.

Put the fish in a crock or glass container. Salt liberally. Add the other ingredients, mix well and cover with fresh-squeezed lime juice. Cover container and marinate overnight in refrigerator. Do not pack tightly in container.

Smoked Fish Spread

1½ pounds smoked fish
 2 tsp. minced onion
 2 tsp. celery, chopped fine
 1 clove garlic, minced
 2 tbsp. sweet pickle relish
 1 cup mayonnaise
 1 tbsp. mustard
 ½ tsp. Worcestershire sauce

Flake the fish and stir all ingredients together thoroughly.

Chill well before serving on crackers. Makes about 3 cups.

To turn this tasty spread into a dip, take a portion of it and thin to desired consistency by slowly stirring in some sour cream.

Fried Fish Bits

Cubes of boneless fish about 1 inch in size

or

Fish cake mixture (from the recipe in this chapter), rolled into small balls about ¾ inch in diameter

If fish cubes are used, salt and pepper them, then dip in beaten egg and cover with Italian-seasoned bread crumbs or corn flake crumbs. Do the same with fish balls, except do not add salt or pepper. Fry for just a minute or so in very hot oil, 400 to 425 degrees. Drain and serve on appetizer table in chafing dish or insulated container. Pick up with toothpicks.

This is nothing more than good old fried fish, always a hit, cooked and served for nibbling instead of dining.

CHOWDERS, SOUPS AND STEWS

From bouillabaisse to catfish stew, fish "soups" are actually hearty main courses which need no accompaniment other than a salad and some bread or crackers. To make any of these dishes, you can start either with boned chunks or fillets, or else with whole dressed fish—stopping to pick out the bones, head and skin after the fish is cooked tender.

New England Chowder

2 pounds fish
Salt pork
3 large potatoes
1 large onion
2 cups milk, cream or half-and-half
Butter, salt and pepper
Water

Start fish simmering in a saucepan with barely enough water to cover. Fry a small piece of salt pork in a skillet. Add diced potatoes and toss. When potatoes are brown add them, and the sliced onion, to the fish. Simmer a few minutes until potatoes and fish are tender. Add milk or cream, and heat to verge of boiling. Add a large pat of butter. Remove and serve. Individuals should salt and pepper their servings to taste.

Fast Chowder for Camp or Home

1 pound fish
4 medium potatoes
1 small onion
1 can evaporated milk
Butter, salt and pepper

Cut potatoes in half and put into saucepan with the sliced onion and the fish. Barely cover with water and boil gently until potatoes are soft when pierced with a fork. Use a large spoon to coarsely mash the fish and potatoes. Stir in a can of evaporated milk and heat to verge of boiling. Add a glob of butter. Salt and pepper to taste, individually.

European Chowder

2 pounds fish
¼ stick butter
1 carrot, diced
1 onion, sliced or chopped
1 tsp. salt
generous sprinkling of black pepper
1 cup white wine

Melt butter in skillet and brown fish, which need not be cooked through. If you use a Dutch oven, proceed in the same vessel; otherwise, transfer fish to saucepan, add other ingredients, bring to boil and boil gently for 5 minutes.

or longer if carrot is not tender. There is no danger of
o much boiling, so unless you're pressed for time, simmer
other 15 minutes. Add the juice of ½ lemon (optional),
r and serve.

tfish Stew, Southern Style

2 slices bacon
1 large onion, chopped
1 large can tomatoes
2 large potatoes, diced
1 tsp. salt
1 cup boiling water
2 tbsp. Worcestershire sauce
⁄4 cup catsup
⁄4 tsp. thyme
⁄4 pounds skinned catfish fillets

In Dutch oven or heavy saucepan, fry bacon, remove,
ain on paper and crumble back into pan with the chopped
ions. Brown onions lightly; then add water, tomatoes and
her ingredients except fish. Simmer for 30 minutes, cov-
ed. Add fish, cut into bite-sized pieces, and simmer 15
ore minutes, uncovered.

ew York Stew

⁄2 cup celery, diced
1 small onion, chopped
1 carrot, chopped
1 large potato, diced
⁄2 pounds cod, halibut or other white fish
⁄2 tsp. garlic salt
our for thickening
⁄2 cup (or small can) shrimp or crabmeat (optional)

Place vegetables in saucepan, barely cover with water,
d boil for 15 minutes. Add fish and garlic salt, with

shrimp, if desired, and simmer another 10 minutes. Thicken
with flour paste, if necessary. Stir to break up fish and
mix well.

Deluxe Stew

   2 pounds fish
   1 onion, sliced
   1 cup white wine
   1 cup mushrooms, sliced
   1 large potato, diced
  ¼ tsp. thyme
   1 small carrot, thinly sliced
  ½ cup celery, chopped
generous sprinkling of salt and pepper

   Sauté fish lightly in a little oil or butter. Add onion slices
and brown. Add wine and other ingredients. Cover and simmer about 15 minutes, or until vegetables are tender. Stir
lightly to break up fish, and thicken with flour paste, if
desired.

French Bouillabaisse

   2 pounds fish fillets
   Other seafoods (choose 2 or 3):
      1 doz. large shrimp, peeled and veined
      1 doz. oysters
      1 pound lobster meat
      6 small scallops
      6 clams in shell
  ½ cup butter
   1 large onion, minced
   1 garlic clove, minced
   2 cups fish stock (made by boiling head and bones of fish)
   1 large ripe tomato, peeled
   1 tsp. salt
   1 lemon, sliced
  ¼ cup red wine

Sauté onion in the butter. Add garlic, fish and other sea-
od (except clams). A large pan or Dutch oven is needed.
uté about 5 minutes until seafood is cooked. Add stock
d other ingredients, and simmer 10 more minutes. Serve
spooning portions of each seafood into bowls, then
dling liquid into each bowl. Float a lemon slice on top.

uick Bouillabaisse

 fish, about 3 or 4 pounds live weight
 stick butter
 onion, minced
1 clove garlic, minced
1 bay leaf
2 cloves
1 tsp. salt
 tsp. black pepper
1 small can tomatoes
1 can shrimp
1 can clams, in shell

Scale and fillet fish, retaining head, skin and bones. Boil
sh parts (except fillets), in enough water to cover, for 20
inutes. Strain. In a large frying pan, sauté onion and
arlic and then brown fish fillets. Add other ingredients
nd fish stock, and simmer for 15 minutes.

This dish can be spiced up by adding ¼ cup cooking
erry and a tablespoon of Worcestershire sauce.

anhattan Fish Chowder

1 pound fish
2 slices bacon or equivalent salt pork
1 small onion, chopped
 green pepper, chopped
1 cup celery, chopped
1 cup fish stock
1 large potato, diced
1 tsp. salt

1 large can tomatoes
½ tsp. pepper

Cut fish into small pieces. Fry bacon until lightly brown
not crisp. Add onion, green pepper and celery. Cook unt
tender. Add rest of ingredients and simmer for about 2
minutes until potatoes are tender.

BAKED FISH RECIPES

As already discussed in Chapter 4, simple baked fish—
whether it be a whole dressed fish stuffed or unstuffe
steaks or fillets—requires little more than salt and som
butter or other fat for basting. But many attractive var
ations are available, and they can add not only changes i
taste, but in texture and appearance as well.

Several recipes for stuffings will be given first.

Rice-Mushroom Stuffing

  ½ cup butter
  1 large onion, minced
  2 cups celery, minced
  1 cup sliced mushrooms
2¼ cups cooked rice
  ½ tsp. each: salt, pepper, sage, thyme

Melt butter, and sauté onion, celery and mushroom
about 3 minutes until soft, but not brown. Add other in
gredients and mix thoroughly.

Bread Stuffing

6 tbsp. melted butter
1 small onion, chopped
1 cup celery, chopped
3 cups dry bread crumbs
1 tsp. each: salt, thyme, sage
Dash of pepper

Sauté onions and celery in butter until soft, not brown. Put crumbs and seasonings in a bowl and add the sautéed vegetables. Toss thoroughly. If dressing seems too dry, add a couple of tablespoons of water to moisten.

Sour Cream Stuffing

¼ cup melted butter
1 small onion, chopped
1 cup celery, chopped
4 cups dry bread cubes
½ cup sour cream
2 tbsp. grated lemon rind
1 tsp. paprika
1 tsp. salt

Cook celery and onion in butter until tender. Combine all ingredients and mix throughly.

Cornbread Stuffing

3 tbsp. melted butter
1 small onion, chopped
1 cup celery, chopped
1 tbsp. lemon juice
½ tsp. salt
2 cups soft bread crumbs
1 cup cornbread, crumbled

Sauté onion and celery in butter until soft. Add other ingredients and toss well, but lightly.

Baked Fillets Hawaiian

Rice-Mushroom stuffing
1 cup crushed pineapple, well drained
2 large fillets, skinned or skin-on
3 slices bacon (optional)

Mix pineapple with stuffing and spread between fillets. If skin is on the fillet, brush top generously with butter before baking at 350 degrees for 30 to 40 minutes. Test for flakiness with fork. If fillet has no skin, you may wish to lay bacon slices across the top to eliminate need for basting.

Baked Fish Alicante

    1 onion, sliced
    1 pound fillets or steaks about 1 inch thick
   ¼ cup olive oil or vegetable oil
   ½ cup brown gravy (from mix if necessary)
   ½ cup white wine
   ¼ tsp. salt
Sprinkling of pepper
   ¼ cup nuts, finely chopped

Spread 3 onion slices in bottom of casserole or foil-lined baking dish. Place fish in dish. Mix other ingredients well and pour over fish. Bake at 350 degrees for 20 to 30 minutes.

Pompano en Papillote

(Also outstanding with sole, or other fine white fish)

1½ cup fish stock
   2 whole pompano, 1 pound each, dressed and drawn, *or* 4 pompano fillets
   1 tbsp. butter
   1 cup crabmeat
   1 cup boiled shrimp, chopped
   1 large onion, chopped
   1 cup sliced mushrooms
   1 tbsp. flour
   2 egg yolks
   ¼ cup white wine
Salt and pepper

Use heads to make fish stock by simmering in small amount of water for 30 minutes. Melt butter in skillet and brown fish at medium heat on both sides. Remove. Sauté crab and shrimp lightly, adding more butter if necessary. Add stock, onion and mushrooms and simmer for 5 minutes. Make a paste with the flour and a little stock. Stir in paste, egg yolks, wine, salt and pepper. Place one whole fish or 2 fillets on half of a large square of parchment paper or aluminum foil. Spoon half the sauce over each. Fold, seal and bake 20 minutes at 450 degrees.

Fillets en Papillote (quick style)

2 pounds fillets
½ cup melted butter
1 tbsp. lemon juice
½ tsp. dill
1 tsp. salt
1 onion, sliced thin
½ pound thin-sliced Swiss cheese

Sprinkle fish with salt and pepper. Combine butter, lemon juice, dill and salt. Cut fillets into 6 equal portions. Cut 6 squares of heavy aluminum foil, 12 inches square. Place 1 tsp. of butter mixture on half of each foil square and lay a serving of fish on top of the sauce, then an onion slice, then another tsp. butter mixture and, finally, a slice of cheese. Seal edges of the foil packets and bake at 400 degrees for about 30 minutes.

Baked Fillets with Crab and Shrimp

3 pounds fillets
Salt and pepper
2 tbsp. butter
2 tbsp. flour
1 cup milk
¼ cup each crabmeat and cooked shrimp, chopped

1 small onion, chopped
¼ cup celery
1 tsp. salt

Sprinkle fish with salt and pepper. Melt butter in pan and stir in flour. Slowly add milk. Stir until smooth and thickened. Remove from heat and stir in other ingredients. Roll up filling inside the fillets, securing with toothpicks. Brush outside of fillets with melted butter. Bake at 400 degress for about 30 minutes, basting twice more.

Baked Fish, Spanish Style

1 large onion, chopped
¼ cup olive oil
1 No. 2½ can tomatoes
2 tbsp. capers
3–oz. jar stuffed olives or olive bits
1 tsp. salt
½ tsp. black pepper
1 tsp. oregano
2 tsp. chili powder (optional)
1 whole dressed fish, about 6 pounds *or* 3–4 pounds of fillets

Sauté onion in olive oil. Add tomatoes and simmer for 5 minutes. Add other ingredients, except fish, and blend. Place fish in foil-lined baking dish. Pour sauce over and bake in 350-degree oven for 30 to 40 minutes. If using whole fish, spoon sauce over fish several times while baking.

Baked Fish Exotica

1 whole fish, dressed—about 6 pounds
¼ cup lime juice
3 cups salted cashew nuts, chopped
¼ pound cheddar cheese, grated

1 small onion, grated
2 bay leaves, crushed
1 cup dry bread crumbs
1 cup milk
½ stick melted butter
¼ cup sherry

Rub fish inside and out with lime juice and sprinkle with salt. Place in foil-lined baking pan. Mix 2½ cups of chopped nuts with the grated cheese, onion, bay leaves and half the bread crumbs. Pour in milk and stir to make a thick paste. Cover fish with paste and sprinkle on the remaining bread crumbs. Bake at 375 degrees for about 45 minutes. In testing for doneness, ease fish up with spatula and test from bottom. Do not break the crust. About three times while fish is baking, dribble mixture of butter and sherry over the top. When done, remove to platter and sprinkle with remaining nuts.

Baked Fillets in Herb Sauce

2 pounds fillets
2 tbsp. cornstarch
¼ cup butter or vegetable oil
1 cup bouillion or fish stock
1 tbsp. catsup
½ tsp. mustard
2 tbsp. chopped onion
1 tsp. salt
½ tsp. pepper
½ cup dry bread crumbs

Put fillets into a foil-lined baking dish. Melt butter and blend in cornstarch. Add bouillon slowly, then cook until smooth, stirring constantly. Add other ingredients, except bread crumbs, gradually while stirring. Pour over fish. Toss bread crumbs with a pat of melted butter and sprinkle over fish. Bake at 350 degrees for 30 to 35 minutes.

Baked Fillets with Sour Cream and Mayonnaise

      2 pounds fillets
1½ cups sour cream
 ½ cup mayonnaise
      2 scallions, chopped
 ½ tsp. salt
 ½ tsp. pepper
      4 tbsp. lime juice

Place fillets on foil-lined baking dish. Mix other ingredients together and spread over fish. Bake at 375 degrees for about 30 minutes.

Festive Baked Fish

      2 pounds fillets
 ½ cup French dressing
1½ cups cheese crackers, crushed
      2 tbsp. oil

Cut fillets into serving-size pieces. Dip fish in dressing and roll in crumbed crackers. Place on foil-lined pan or cookie sheet. Drizzle oil over fish. Bake quickly in 500-degree oven for 10 to 12 minutes. Test with fork.

Baked Fish, Fast but Fancy

2 pounds fillets or steaks
Salt and pepper
1 can condensed soup

Place fillets in foil-lined baking pan and sprinkle with salt and pepper. Pour soup (any kind, according to your taste or mood—tomato, mushroom, celery, shrimp, cheddar cheese) into bowl and stir it well. Add a bit of milk to thin it a little if desired, but don't mix in another whole can of liquid as the directions on the can prescribe. Pour soup over fish. Bake in a 400-degree oven about 30 minutes or until tender.

If soup doesn't cover fish entirely, baste frequently during cooking.

SAUTÉED FISH RECIPES

Sautéing, or pan-frying, is suitable for steaks, fillets or small whole panfish. With variation in sauces, the possibilities for subtle changes are virtually endless.

A few panfish which are especially good for sautéing with special sauces are crappie, white bass, grunts and small snapper. But many can be used—including, of course, the famous pompano and small trout.

Sauté Amandine

Fish
Flour for dredging
Butter, margarine or oil for cooking
Salt and pepper
Almonds, bleached and sliced
Lemon juice

Dredge fish in flour, with salt and pepper. Cover pan with a little oil—up to about ½ inch. Sauté fish in oil at medium heat until brown, turning once. Remove. Add sliced almonds and a little butter to same pan, after draining away oil. Stir until almonds are light brown. Pour almonds over fish and sprinkle with lemon. For three persons, use ½ cup almonds.

Spicy Sauté Amandine

2 pounds fillets
1 egg
1 cup milk
Flour
½ cup butter
¼ cup almonds, sliced
2 tbsp. Worcestershire sauce
Juice of 2 lemons

99

Salt and pepper fish. Beat egg and milk together. Dip fish in egg-milk mixture and dredge in flour. In skillet, melt butter and sauté fish at medium heat until brown on both sides. Remove fish. Add almonds to skillet and brown. Add lemon juice and Worcestershire sauce. Pour over fish.

Sautéed Trout, Russian Style

    6 to 8 small stream trout, dressed
    2 eggs, beaten
    ½ cup milk
    1½ cups prepared bread crumbs, fine
    Oil for frying
    1 stick butter, soft
    2 hard-boiled eggs, chopped
    2 tbsp. pimiento, chopped
    Salt and pepper

Salt and pepper trout. Mix eggs and milk; dip trout in mixture, then roll in bread crumbs. Sauté in skillet at medium heat, using just a light covering of oil. Make a paste of the butter, eggs and pimiento. Spread paste over hot fish and serve immediately.

Sautéed Smoked Fish with Eggs

Smoked fish fillets or small pieces
1 tbsp. butter
Eggs, beaten with salt, pepper and a little milk

If serving-size pieces of smoked fish are used, sauté them in butter at medium-low temperature just long enough to heat well, turning once. Remove fish and scramble eggs in the same pan.

If small bits of smoked fish are used, simply mix them with the beaten eggs and scramble all together.

Sautéed Fish in Sour Cream

2 pounds fillets or steaks
Flour
Salt and pepper
½ tsp. basil, crushed
1 cup sour cream
¼ cup butter or oil
1 onion, sliced

Cut fish into serving-size portions. Sauté onion in butter until tender. Sauté fish at medium heat, turning once, until golden brown on both sides. Cover fish with onion, basil and sour cream. Cover and simmer gently for 5 minutes or until fish meets test for doneness.

BROILED FISH

In flavor, broiled fish is almost identical to baked fish, and many of the recipes also are similar. The chief differ-ence, of course, is that broiled fish is cooked for shorter periods at high temperatures. Many sauces add zest and variety.

Broiled Steaks au Gratin

4 fish steaks, about ½ inch thick
Butter
1 cup bread crumbs
½ cup cheddar cheese, grated (other kinds may be used)
Salt and pepper

Place steaks in foil-lined baking pan. Brush with melted butter. Sprinkle on bread crumbs and grated cheese until each steak is covered. Broil about 10 minutes. Salt and pepper to taste.

Spicy Broiled Fish

    2 pounds fillets
  ½ cup steak sauce
  ¼ cup catsup
  ¼ cup vegetable oil
    1 tbsp. vinegar
    1 tsp. salt
  ½ tsp. curry powder

Place fish, skin-side up on foil-lined broiler pan, and spread with sauce made of other six ingredients. Broil about 3 inches from broiler unit for 5 minutes. Turn fish carefully and spread other side with sauce. Broil until fish flakes when tested with fork.

Broiled Fish Steak au Vin

Fish steaks, about ¾ inch thick
Salt and pepper
Butter
White wine

Place steaks in foil-lined pan and sprinkle with salt and pepper. Place under broiler for a couple of minutes until surface of fish is hot. Remove and brush each piece with a pat of butter held on a fork. Return to broiler and cook two minutes. Remove again, spread more butter and splash liberally with white wine. Return to finish cooking, about 3 minutes. Sprinkle on a little more wine before serving.

Quick and Spicy Broiled Fillets

    2 pounds fillets
Salt and pepper
Lime juice
  ½ cup French dressing

Place fillets in foil-lined baking dish. Sprinkle with salt, pepper and lime juice. Pour on the French dressing. Broil until done—about 5 or 10 minutes, according to thickness.

NOTE: Either for convenience or added flavor from marinating, this dish can be prepared as instructed and placed in your refrigerator for anywhere from an hour to several hours before cooking. Broiling time will increase slightly.

Deviled Broiled Fillets

2 pounds fillets
½ cup chili sauce
2 tbsp. mustard
1 tbsp. Worcestershire sauce
½ tsp. salt
¼ tsp. pepper

Place fillets in foil-lined pan. Mix all other ingredients and spread over fish. Broil for about 5 minutes until done.

Broiled Fish Steaks, Oriental

2 pounds fish steaks
¼ cup orange juice
¼ cup soy sauce
2 tbsp. catsup
2 tbsp. oil
1 tbsp. lemon juice
½ tsp. oregano
½ tsp. pepper
1 clove garlic, finely chopped

Place fish in a foil-lined baking dish. Combine remaining ingredients and pour over fish; let stand for 30 minutes, turning once. Remove and reserve sauce for basting. Place fish under broiler and broil about 4 to 5 minutes on each side, basting liberally with sauce at least twice on each side.

POACHED FISH RECIPES

The procedure for poaching fish is given in Chapter 4. The following recipes are for sauces and garnishes that go on after the fish is poached.

Most of the famous poached fish recipes deal with sole or salmon. But substitute any choice fish you have.

Although fish can be poached in salted water, the tastiest results are obtained by poaching them in a court bouillon. This is made at the time of use—never stockpiled in advance.

Court Bouillon

3 cups water
1 onion, sliced
¼ cup vinegar
½ tsp. salt
½ tsp. black pepper
1 bay leaf
¼ tsp. thyme

Put all ingredients in pan. Stir. Bring to a boil and simmer at least 30 minutes before cooking fish.

Court Bouillon with Wine

2 cups water
2 cups white wine
½ tsp. salt
½ tsp. pepper
½ lemon, sliced

Combine all ingredients, bring to a boil, and add fish immediately.

Court Bouillon Deluxe

1/4 cup each of carrots, celery and onion, chopped
  2 tbsp. butter
  1 cup red wine
1/2 tsp. salt
1/2 tsp. black pepper

Sauté the vegetables in the butter until soft, not brown. Add other ingredients and boil 15 minutes before cooking fish.

Poached Fish Hollandaise

2 pounds fish fillets
Court bouillon
Hollandaise Sauce
Lemon slices

Poach fillets in court bouillon, remove to platter and cover with Hollandaise sauce. Garnish with lemon slices. As to the Hollandaise sauce, you're on your own. I get someone else to make mine.

Poached Fish Mariniere

  2 pounds filet of sole or other mild fish
Court bouillon
  1 cup scallions, chopped
1/2 cup butter
  3 tbsp. flour
  2 cups milk
1/2 tsp. salt
1/2 cup white wine
  2 egg yolks, beaten

Poach fish in court bouillon and remove to platter. Sauté

scallions in butter. Blend in flour and stir constantly while heating, 3 or 4 minutes. Add milk and stir until smooth. Add salt and wine; simmer 5 minutes more. Remove from heat and stir in egg yolks. Spoon sauce over fish.

Poached Fish with Mushrooms

2 pounds fish fillets
Wine-style court bouillon
1 onion, chopped *or* 2-3 scallions, chopped
Butter
1 small can mushroom slices
1 can condensed cream of mushroom soup

Poach fish in court bouillon and remove to platter. In skillet, brown onion or scallions in a little butter. Add the mushroom slices and soup. Stir until smooth. Add some of the court bouillon—a little at a time—stirring constantly until desired consistency is obtained. Ordinarily, less than a cup of the court bouillon is used. Pour sauce over poached fish.

Poached Fish with Oysters

1½ pounds fish fillets
Court bouillon
  1 egg yolk
  2 scallions, chopped
Juice of ¼ lemon
 12 raw oysters

Poach fish in court bouillon and remove to platter. Cool one cup of the court bouillon and mix in the well-beaten egg yolk, scallions and lemon juices. Simmer for 3 minutes, add oysters, and simmer 3 more minutes. Pour over fish and serve.

Poached Trout Normandy

2 large fillets of trout or salmon, up to 2 pounds each
Court bouillon
½ stick butter
1 onion, chopped
¼ cup flour
½ cup white wine
1 pound boiled shrimp, *or* 1 can shrimp
2 hard-boiled eggs
Salt and pepper to taste

Poach fish in court bouillon and remove to platter, re-serving bouillon. Sauté the onion in the butter. Blend in the flour. Add one cup of the court bouillon and the wine. Simmer 5 minutes. Chop shrimp and eggs, and stir lightly into sauce. Pour sauce over fish.

Poached Fish Supreme, with Wine

1½ pounds fish steaks or fillets—salmon or trout preferred;
    white-meat fish almost as good
Fish stock or deluxe court bouillon
½ stick butter
2 scallions, chopped
¼ cup flour
½ tsp. each, salt and pepper
1 egg yolk
½ cup white wine
2 cups mashed potatoes, prepared and seasoned

Poach fish in bouillon or stock and remove to platter, re-serving liquid. Sauté scallions in butter and sprinkle in the flour, blending well. Blend in 2 cups of the fish stock or court bouillon, salt and pepper. Heat until steaming but not boiling. Beat egg yolk and wine together and stir into the hot sauce. Remove from heat. Make a ridge of mashed potatoes all around the fish on the platter. Pour souce over fish and place under hot broiler until potatoes start to brown. Remove and serve immediately.

LEFTOVER OR FLAKED FISH

Leftover fish can be flaked and used in many different ways, but most of the following recipes are so good you may want to poach some fish and make them without waiting for leftovers to turn up.

It makes no difference whether the leftover fish is fried, boiled, broiled, poached or baked. If it's fried, remove as much of the coating as possible before flaking.

Baked Fish Loaf

   1 chicken bouillon cube
   1 cup boiling water
   2 cups flaked fish
1½ cups bread cubes
   2 eggs, beaten
  ½ cup celery, chopped
  ½ cup milk or light cream
   1 tsp. onion, grated
   1 tsp. salt
   2 tsp. lemon juice

Put bouillon cube in water and stir until cube dissolves. Add all other ingredients, mix well, and place in a greased loaf pan. Bake at 350 degrees for about an hour, or until loaf is firm in the center. Serves 6.

Fish Newburg

   2 egg yolks
   1 tbsp. cornstarch
1½ cups milk

        2 cups flaked fish
Salt and pepper
Dash of nutmeg
        2 tbsp. butter
        4 tbsp. sherry

Beat egg yolks with cornstarch until light. Gradually add milk, stirring constantly. Put into top of double boiler (or use a chafing dish) with the fish. Add salt, pepper and nutmeg—all lightly. Cook over briskly boiling water until sauce is quite thick. Add butter and sherry and stir. Serve on rice or toast.

Fish and Mushroom Pie

        1 cup pastry mix
        3 slices bacon
1¼ cups milk, scalded
        1 tsp. onion, grated
    ½ tsp. salt
        3 eggs, beaten
        2 cups flaked fish
        1 can mushrooms, drained (4 oz.)

Prepare pastry mix and line a pie pan. Fry bacon until crisp; drain. To scalded milk add onion and salt. Add the hot milk slowly to beaten eggs, stirring constantly. Spread fish over pie shell. Spread mushrooms over fish. Pour in the milk-egg mixture, and sprinkle crumbled bacon over the top. Bake in 425-degree oven for 20 minutes. Reduce heat and bake about 15 minutes longer until pie is firm in center.

Flaked Fish Soufflé

        3 eggs
        1 cup milk
        2 cups flaked fish
        1 cup fish stock

1 small onion, grated
3 tbsp. vinegar
1 tsp. salt
½ tsp. pepper

Separate egg yolks and whip the whites. Beat the egg yolks and stir in the milk; add everything else except the egg whites and mix well. Fold in the egg whites. Pour into a casserole or glass (Pyrex) bowl. Set in a pan of water and bake at 300 degrees about 45 minutes. Test by inserting a knife in the center. If it comes out clean, fish is done.

Creamy Flaked Fish Casserole

2 cups flaked fish
½ tsp. salt
2 tbsp. lemon juice
1 tbsp. butter
1 can tomato soup
2 cups mashed potatoes

Mix fish with salt and lemon juice. Add butter to soup and heat, stirring until smooth. Do not boil. Add fish and mix. Pour into shallow casserole or baking dish. Top with mashed potatoes. Place under broiler for a few minutes until potatoes brown.

Fish Cakes

3 large potatoes
¼ stick butter
Salt and pepper
1 egg
½ cup evaporated milk
1 cup flaked fish

Boil potatoes; drain and mash thoroughly. Add butter, some salt and pepper, and blend by stirring. Beat egg and milk together and add to potatoes. Beat until light and fluffy. Add the fish and beat again. Form into balls of desired size, or drop from tablespoon, and fry in deep fat at 375 to 400 degrees.

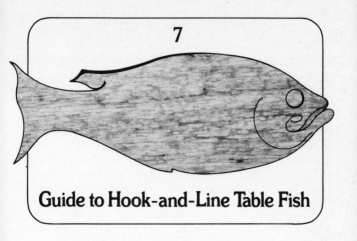

7

Guide to Hook-and-Line Table Fish

The following lists provide a quick reference to all the major hook-and-line food fish of North American waters, fresh and salt, with notes concerning their table quality, preferred methods of dressing and preferred methods of cooking.

Various popular and regional names are listed, many of which are merely cross-referenced. In cases where closely related species are involved, the commentary for all is given under a single heading: for instance, the trouts, basses and groupers.

This section is designed to answer those famous questions: "Is this fish good to eat?" and "How should I cook it?" Once you check the list, and get on the right track, you'll find detailed instructions on cleaning and cooking methods in other chapters.

Please note that this listing is in no way intended as a guide to identification of the fish.

No doubt you've seen books or pamphlets which attempt to rate the *taste* of the different species by some such notations as "Excellent" or "Fair." That sort of flat categorization has been deliberately ignored here, because the author feels that *any* fish worth the bother is highly enjoyable. The few that should not be bothered with are duly noted.

113

FRESHWATER FISH

BASS, BLACK. This group includes the largemouth and smallmouth bass, plus several closely-related species such as the spotted or Kentucky bass, redeye bass, Suwannee bass and Guadalupe bass. All can be treated alike. The largemouth is widely regarded as the poorest eating of the lot, but this isn't necessarily so. The largemouth does often have a "muddy" odor and taste, particularly if taken in still, mud-bottomed waters. Since smallmouths and the other species are usually taken in clear or flowing waters, this odd taste is encountered only in a rare very large specimen, and is never pronounced even then. In defense of the largemouth, though, it is unlikely you'll notice any difference between species of similar size caught in similar waters. And, in any event, a largemouth bass which is filleted and skinned loses the objectionable taste.

Bass meat is white, firm and lean. Large specimens are inclined to coarseness. Fish of one pound and up should be filleted and skinned. Smaller specimens are delicious when scaled and treated as panfish. They also can be scaled and baked whole, but watch out for that muddy taste if a big largemouth is so treated.

BASS, ROCK. This name is widely used for the striped bass (see below). The common freshwater rock bass is another species entirely, similar to the warmouth and usually prepared as panfish (which see).

BASS, STRIPED. The saltwater striped bass is now a freshwater staple in many different lakes where it has been introduced. It's also called rock bass, rockfish or simply "rock."

The meat is lean and white, suitable for any of the preparation methods you might prefer. The fish can be scaled and filleted, skinned and filleted, or prepared whole.

BASS, WHITE. This is a close relative of the striped bass, and equally good. It can be treated as striped bass, but is usually of panfish size and should be so handled. Larger ones can be scaled and filleted or skinned and filleted.

BASS, YELLOW. Another related species, it is treated as for white bass.

BLUEGILL. See Panfish.

BREAM. See Panfish.

BUFFALO. A sometimes-huge member of the sucker family, buffalo fish are not highly prized, but can be prepared as for carp (which see).

BULLHEAD. See Catfish.

CARP. Small specimens can be quite good and lend themselves to a variety of cooking methods. Carp of any size should be skinned. Large ones are coarse, but good when the meat is boiled and then ground or flaked, and used in chowders or as ground fish for fish cakes and similar uses.

CATFISH. This is a large family and though most are called catfish of one kind or another, you'll hear other names, such as "bullhead" and "pout." Some types, such as the channel catfish and blue catfish, have better table reputations than others, but all are excellent eating. Any difference in flavor is due more to the water in which they are caught than to their species.

All catfish should be skinned, and special instructions are given in Chapter Two. Best of all are the little fellows, deep-fried whole. Catfish of between one and six pounds should be filleted after skinning, and the fillets cut into the proper size pieces for frying, or for chowder. Very big catfish can be coarse and sometimes strong. Serving-size pieces cut from big catfish can be fried, but you'll probably like them better in chowders or stews, or baked with sauces.

CHAR. See Trout.

CHUB. Several types of small fish are called chub. Most common is the eastern chub or "fallfish," which averages around eight inches or so, and is good but bony. Scale and dress as for panfish, then score the sides several times with a knife and deep-fry. Scoring helps soften the bones.

CISCO. See Whitefish.

CRAPPIE. See Panfish.

DRUM. Also called sheepshead. This fellow is inclined to coarseness. Small ones are pretty good scaled and baked. Others should be skinned and the meat used for chowder.

EEL. The common eel, although born in the sea, is almost always caught in fresh water and considered a freshwater fish. And a fish it is, despite its snake-like appearance. Clean eels the same way you would catfish (see Chapter Two). Make a cut through the skin all the way around the head. Then peel the skin off with pliers. It will help to nail the head to a board, as with catfish. Smoked and pickled eels are famous delicacies of two continents. You'll like them, too, simply chopped into pieces and fried.

FALLFISH. See Chub.

GRAYLING. Though not related, the grayling usually is thought of in connection with trout—and the association extends to the dining department. They are handled and prepared similarly to pan-sized trout, although the scales are much larger and best scraped off. In taste appeal they are at least equal to trout, and many anglers like them better. They can be pan-fried, poached or broiled.

MUSKELLUNGE. Muskies make fine food. Since even a "small" keeper muskie is big, many are baked—with or without stuffing. Though the scales are small in comparison to the size of the fish, some folks like to scrape them before drawing and preparing, although this is optional. The muskie can also be filleted (and skinned if you prefer), then cut into small pieces for frying or broiling. Also, one muskie could be cut in half—or even in chunks—and each half or piece baked as desired.

PANFISH. We're lumping a lot of different small freshwater fish here—all the sunfish family (called "bream" in the South), plus crappies, perch and the smaller basses. All are excellent food fish and prepared the same way, although you can easily tell a difference in the taste of, say, a crappie and a bluegill.

Instructions for dressing panfish are given in Chapter

Two. After cleaning, they are most commonly fried in deep fat, but can just as easily be pan-fried or broiled.

Bluegills, shellcrackers and other sunfish, along with rock bass and warmouth, sometimes develop a "muddy" taste—especially when they reach sizes approaching a pound and are taken from still or murky water. If you do notice such a disagreeable taste in your larger panfish, it can be removed simply by skinning the fish. You can either skin the fish without filleting it, or you can fillet and then skin. Instructions on both methods are found in Chapter Two.

Also, when frying larger panfish whole you may find it advisable to score each side two or three times. This allows the thicker portions to become properly cooked in a short time.

PERCH, SPECKLED. Another name for crappie. See Panfish.

PERCH, WHITE. See Panfish. Also, the white perch is sometimes large enough to prepare whole for baking. It's good all ways.

PERCH, YELLOW. See Panfish.

PICKEREL. Though unbelievably bony, pickerel are delicious, the meat fine and white. In larger members of this family—the pike and muskellunge—the myriad bones are large enough to be picked out. This is almost an impossible job with the pickerel. Try this: fillet the pickerel, leaving the skin on; lay skin side down on a cutting board, and with a sharp knife slash the meat of each fillet *many times*, close together, from one end of the fillet to the other. Do not cut through the skin (some cuts through the skin can't be avoided and are all right so long as the fillet holds together).

Now cut each fillet into serving-size pieces and deep-fry them. The bones will have been cut even smaller, and further softened by frying. They can be eaten along with the meat.

Pickerel have very small scales which are hard to scrape off. Many people don't bother to do so.

117

PIKE, NORTHERN. This fish is very bony, as are its relatives, the muskie and pickerel. For specimens up to seven or eight pounds, follow directions given for pickerel. Big ones can be treated as muskie, since the bones are large enough to be picked out—which can be a demanding job, but not impossible and certainly worthwhile.

PIKE, REDFIN. Common in only a few areas, the redfin pike is a little fellow, seldom exceeding a few inches. The scales are so small you can ignore them—and so are those infamous bones of the pike family. Just cut off the head, draw, wash and fry. Delicious.

PUMPKINSEED. See Panfish.

REDBREAST BREAM. See Panfish.

REDEYE. This name is given to certain black bass species —see Bass, Black. Another fish called redeye is a small sunfish—see Panfish.

ROCKFISH or ROCK. See Striped Bass.

SALMON. This group includes the Atlantic salmon of the North Atlantic and its rivers; landlocked salmon and ouananiche salmon, which are strictly freshwater strains of the Atlantic salmon; and several varieties of Pacific salmon, including the king or chinook and the coho, both of which have been introduced to the Great Lakes.

In their prime, all salmon are famous food fish, and arguments concerning which species are best are mostly opinion. But note that phrase "in their prime." This means fish taken from the sea (or lakes), and stream fish in the early stages of their spawning runs. The longer salmon stay in a stream, the more their flesh deteriorates. But the change in flesh quality is obvious to the eye. Because of this, and because of seasonal knowledge in salmon country, nobody is apt to get stuck with a bad salmon on the table.

Salmon have small scales which are usually ignored, but can be scraped off if you like. The fish then generally is steaked (see instructions in Chapter Two) and the steaks either broiled, baked or poached. Whole salmon of appropriate size may also be baked or poached in a large steaming-vessel. For smoking, salmon should be filleted. Poached salmon may be eaten hot with lemon or a mild sauce, or cold with mayonnaise or another sauce of your choice.

In good salmon-fishing country, there is often a handy cannery where your fish can be canned for a fee or on a share basis.

Landlocked salmon are normally much smaller than the other species and can be treated as for trout. Legal-size salmon of any species which may be too large for the pan, but too small for convenient steaking, can be filleted and prepared as above—broiled or poached.

SAUGER. Often confused with the walleye, the confusion is appropriate when dinner time arrives. The sauger is equally delicious (better, say some), with fine, sweet flesh. Scale and fillet without skinning, then fry or broil. Or you can bake a whole dressed sauger.

SHAD. Most of the raves go to the roe of this fish, but the flesh can also be a gourmet's delight—if you get rid of those bothersome bones. And the simple procedure for doing so is outlined in Chapter Two. In the same chapter, see instructions for turning out a "butterfly" fillet—that is, both fillets cut from the fish but left joined on the underside. If you wish to bake your shad, use the butterfly fillet. Bone each fillet individually, then fold the two fillets back together with stuffing in between. For broiled shad, the fillets can be cut off separately and boned. In any case, scale and behead the shad first. The skin should not be removed.

There are several species of shad in North America. All are good *if* they are large enough, the larger the better. It isn't much use to fool with a shad under a pound at the very least. The common shad, which is the subject of most angling attention, averages three or four pounds.

SHEEPSHEAD. See Drum.

SHELLCRACKER. See Panfish.

SMELT. Eat these little fellows like peanuts, but enjoy them a lot more. Cut off the heads, draw and scrape. Deep-

fry them and eat bones and all if the smelt are tiny ones
If the bones aren't all that tender, eat the meat away from
them as with other panfish.

SQUAWFISH. Like the chub of Eastern rivers, the squaw
fish is an overgrown minnow, and not held in high esteem
by anglers. But it is edible. Treat small ones as for panfish
Larger ones can be scaled and filleted. They are best fried

STEELHEAD. See Trout.

STUMPKNOCKER. See Panfish.

STURGEON. Few anglers are likely ever to see a sturgeon
despite the fact that the great fish occurs in many parts of
the country. When a sturgeon is caught it usually is cut
into small pieces and smoked, but the flesh is quite good
when fried, broiled, baked or used in chowder. A sturgeon
can be skinned, then filleted and the fillets cut into usable
size pieces; or the fish can be steaked.

SUCKER. The several species of sucker are relished by
many people in various parts of the country. The meat is
sweet but bony. Preparing as for pickerel will help. Sucker
are generally scaled and filleted, but sometimes have a
muddy taste. If so, they should be filleted and skinned. Fry
ing is the rule. Sucker meat is quite good when boiled, the
bones picked out, and the flesh used for fish cakes or in
recipes calling for flaked fish.

SUNFISH. See Panfish.

TROUT. Almost all cold, unpolluted waters of North
America hold trout of one kind or another—natural or in
troduced, native or hatchery-stocked. All are among the
most prized of table fish, but there are definite levels of de
sirability—reminiscent of graded beef.

To begin with, hatchery fish are lowest on the list. But
unless you have a taste mechanism tuned to long years of
getting your choice, don't let this bother you, because
hatchery trout are delicious. It's just that natives are even
more delicious.

Naturally, there are preferences by species, too. And jus

s naturally, these preferences do vary among individuals. ut it's a safe bet that the eastern trout fan will prefer rookies to rainbows or browns, while his western counter-art will take cutthroats or brookies over the same pair of ame, but often maligned, species. But readers who al-eady have their own ideas about the eating of trout won't e swayed by any words printed here, anyway. As for the st of you, be assured that you'll enjoy any trout that races your table.

As to handling and preparation, both are covered at ngth in other chapters. By way of summation, small trout ould be slit and drawn, gills removed, and the fish pan-ied, poached or baked. They can also be split and broiled. emove the head if you prefer.

Some trout can get very large in big water. These include ot only the sea-run rainbows called steelhead, but land-cked rainbows in large lakes. Brown trout, too, can ex-ed twenty pounds in lakes. The Dolly Varden grows to age size, as does, of course, the lake trout.

If you're lucky enough to get one of those giants—and ou don't prefer to hang him on the wall—he can be treated s for salmon.

WARMOUTH. See Panfish.

WHITEFISH. Great Lakes whitefish, lake cisco and moun-in whitefish are related species which can be treated the me. All are excellent eating. Scale and prepare as for anfish, or scale and fillet, or split. Delicious and well own as smoked fish, whitefish are also good fried, broiled baked.

SALTWATER FISH

ALBACORE. See Tuna.

AMBERJACK. This fish is very good, though few anglers em to realize it. Fillet the fish and skin the fillets as de-ribed for extra-large fish in Chapter Two. Then "steak" ch of the fillets into serving-size pieces. Trim off any red rtions. Prepare any way you like—fried, broiled, chow-

dered, baked in a sauce of some kind. You may find para
sites in the flesh near the tail, but seldom in other areas
Cut out the infested portion and discard. Parasites are com
mon in most species of fish, but noticeable in only a few
so don't let them bother you. They are harmless when th
fish is cooked.

ANGELFISH. So-so as food, angelfish can be skinne
and filleted, then fried or used in chowder.

BARRACUDA. Several species of barracuda exist, o
which the best known are the Pacific variety and the grea
barracuda of the South Atlantic and Caribbean. Both c
those merit raves on the table, but care must be taken whe
eating the Florida or Bahamas species. On rare occasion
they are afflicted with a poison called ciguatera. Unfortu
nately, there is no way to test whether any particular spec
men might be so afflicted; however, the poison seems to b
encountered only in larger fish from deep water. Fish of fiv
pounds or less, from the Florida flats or inshore waters, ar
safe—and good. Ciguatera poisoning is rarely fatal, but i
painful and lingering—so don't take chances with big ba
racuda.

Pacific barracuda—the species so common off the Cal
fornia coast—is never poisonous. The great barracuda als
occurs in the South Pacific, but not in California waters.

Barracudas are easily filleted and skinned and this is b
far the best way to prepare them. Any red meat may b
trimmed away, although it doesn't seem to impair the tast
Fillets can be cooked in any way you like. They are mil
and lean.

BASS, WHITE SEA. A member of the sea trout genus tha
includes, in Pacific waters, the various corbina species, thi
great fish is the favorite of many, and lends itself to jus
about any type of cleaning or cooking. Fish of appropriat
size may be scaled and prepared for baking. They can b
filleted and skinned, and with the big ones it's best to do
this way. Few fish are better when fried, but you can coo
them any way you prefer. The meat is mild, but flavorfu
and white.

122

BASS, CALIFORNIA BLACK. This huge fish is much like the jewfish or other very large groupers. Generally, it is so big you can only peel the skin off and cut out chunks of meat, butchering them to desired size. Best used in chowers or casseroles, or baked in a sauce, the meat can be fried if cut in thin slices.

BASS, CHANNEL. See Redfish.

BASS, SEA. The common sea bass is also called black bass or blackfish in certain areas of the Atlantic and Gulf coasts. Most of them are small, but these are one of the sweetest of all panfish. Scale and dress as for other panfish. Occasional ones are large enough to skin and fillet, or even to bake. The meat is fine-grained and white.

BASS, GIANT SEA. See Jewfish; also Bass, California Black.

BASS, KELP. Along with the rock bass and sand bass, which are closely related and often confused, the kelp bass is a good food fish of the California coast. Prepare whole for baking, or fillet and skin for frying or broiling.

BASS, ROCK. See above.

BASS, SAND. See above.

BASS, STRIPED. See same in freshwater listings.

BLACKFISH. See Tautog.

BLUEFISH. Delicious but very rich and oily, the bluefish should be put on ice immediately and eaten as soon as possible after it has left the water. They're best the first day, but can be kept several days if well iced and kept drained. Small "snapper blues" are marvelous panfish, dressed and pan-fried. Larger ones can be filleted "buttery fashion" as described in Chapter Two, and the fillets stuffed and baked. Or fillets can be cut singly, without scaling or skinning, and broiled. Skinned fillets are good fried. Whole blues of appropriate size can be dressed and baked.

BLUE RUNNER. See Jack.

BLOWFISH. See Puffer.

BONEFISH. Sportsmen hold that bonefish should be re
leased instead of eaten. But if a bonefish is killed, for on
reason or another, it can make a great dinner. The onl
problem is—you guessed it—bones. Fillet the bonefish but
terfly fashion (see Chapter Two). Broil the double fillet
skin side down. When done, a great many bones will "arch
up" from the meat. Pick these away carefully and then di
in—but cautiously, because more bones remain in the flesh
The flesh, though, is fat and quite tasty, and needs nothin
more than some salt and lemon.

BONITO. See Tuna.

BREAM. Various saltwater panfish are called bream, a
though no particular one really owns the name. Prepare a
for grunts.

BUTTERFISH. This is a generally large panfish, whic
can be scaled and dressed whole for baking, or scaled an
filleted for frying or broiling. Very tasty.

CABEZONE. One of the largest members of the sculpi
family, the Pacific cabezone is best when filleted an
skinned. Though not much for looks, the fish is quite goo
eating.

CATFISH. Unlike their freshwater relatives, saltwater ca
fish are not highly prized as table fare. The common se
catfish is edible but rather strong tasting. The gafftopsa
catfish is bigger, gamer, and better to eat as well—havin
pinkish flesh which is good fried, and great in chowders c
stews. Unfortunately, the gafftopsail is covered with a thic
slime which makes skinning a distasteful chore. Skin sal
water catfish the same way as freshwater catfish (see Chap
ter Two).

COBIA. By whatever name it's known, the cobia is an un
usual and excellent food fish—unusual because most agre
it doesn't taste "like fish." The flavor has been likened t
chicken or frog legs. Some other names for the cobia: lin
cabbeo, sergeantfish, crabeater.

Even small cobia have thick, sharklike skin. These should be filleted and then skinned. Large fish can be skinned first, then filleted, and the fillets cut into steaks. Or they can be steaked without filleting. In small pieces, cobia is delicious fried. Large chunks and steaks can be broiled or baked. Meat is dry so use sauce or butter while cooking.

COD. Little need be said about the table qualities of the cod. Most caught these days are smallish and best filleted, either with or without skinning. Butterfly fillets, with skin left on, are the kind you see for salted cod. Salt cod is a staple in many parts of the world, but fresh cod is *out* of this world. Broil, bake, chowder or cake, you can hardly find a bad way to cook fresh cod.

COD, ROCK. See Rockfish.

COD, TOM. See Tomcod.

CONEY. See Grouper.

CORBINA. This name is applied to various members of the weakfish or sea trout genus of Pacific waters, and also to the California corbina, which is of the same family but more closely resembles the croakers. Regardless, they are all among the best table fish of the Pacific, and prime favorites throughout the tropical Americas. The meat is mild, white, fine-grained. Scale and prepare whole for baking; scale and fillet; fillet and skin. Suit yourself. And cook any way you like. Corbina is the fish usually chosen for making Seviche (see Chapter Six).

CROAKER. Many types of croaker are found along the Atlantic, Pacific and Gulf Coasts. All are very good. Usually pan-size, they should be scaled and dressed whole. Sometimes, however, they reach two pounds or more and can be dressed whole for baking, or filleted. They're excellent fried, baked or broiled.

CUNNER. This is a tasty panfish. Most people like to remove the skin before frying.

DOLPHIN. This deepwater fish occurs around the world and is a choice table variety everywhere. It should be

125

skinned first and then filleted—not vice versa. The fillets are best when baked or broiled, but are also good fried. Keep dolphin well iced, as they grow soft quickly.

DRUM, BLACK. When small—around five pounds or less—black drum are surprisingly good, especially if filleted, skinned and fried. Up to perhaps ten pounds they are good scaled, dressed and baked. Let the giant ones go.

DRUM, RED. See Redfish.

EEL. See listing in Freshwater section.

FLATFISH. Lumped together in this category are all the "doormats"—those strange-looking but invariably excellent tasting fish which are flat and have both eyes on the same, upper, side. Included are the giant halibuts of Atlantic and Pacific, the small dabs, the flounders, flukes and soles. Names are often confused. Several kinds are often represented as "sole" on restaurant menus, and seldom if ever is a customer the wiser.

The rib cavity, encompassing the entrails, is quite small on all flatfish. To clean, simply cut off the head, make a small slit below and remove the entrails. Some cooks prefer to leave the head on, in which case the gills should be removed. Scales on most flatfish are relatively small, though large enough on bigger fish to warrant scaling. Seldom is a flatfish skinned.

Small specimens can be left whole after cleaning, and then can be fried, broiled, baked or pan-fried.

Larger fish can be steaked—although since the fish is flat, the steaks are cut wide and really could be called chunks.

Big specimens also can be filleted with a long knife, and the fillets cut into suitable pieces for broiling, frying, or for baking with a stuffing.

FLOUNDER. See Flatfish.

FLUKE. See Flatfish.

GREENLING. Two Pacific Coast species share this name. One is the true greenling, a small fish of less than two feet

The other is the lingcod, which is sometimes called green-ling because its flesh is green! The lingcod can grow quite large, perhaps as big as a hundred pounds.

Though not closely related, both are popular food fish and should be filleted and skinned. The green flesh of the ling-cod is disconcerting but not harmful.

GROUPER. The groupers are a big clan, covering many species from the giant jewfish and Warsaw grouper to tiny coneys. Those of primary interest to anglers—both as prey and as table fare—fall into two main groupings, or genera, as follows:

Genus *Mycteroperca*, represented in the South Atlantic and Gulf by such species as the black, yellowfin, gag and scamp, and in Lower California by such types as the golden and broomtail. This bunch is rather streamlined, as group-ers go, and, more important for our immediate purposes, somewhat better eating—being finer grained.

Genus *Epinephelus*, represented in the Atlantic by such groupers as the red, Nassau and hinds, and in Mexican Pacific waters by the cabrillas. These are less streamlined, more potbellied than the above group and of coarser flesh.

All groupers are usually filleted and skinned, although it's quite all right to draw and prepare them whole for bak-ing. In that case, there is no need to scale, since the tough skin will not be eaten anyway.

Small groupers of any kind provide fillets which are ex-cellent fried. Large groupers of the genus *Mycteroperca* are also quite good for frying if the fillets are sliced rather thin.

All types are great for chowders and stews, while large fillets, or chunks of large fillets, are excellent if baked in a sauce.

GRUNT. These are among the best of saltwater panfish, being preferred by many old-time Floridians to snapper. Scale and prepare them whole for pan-frying. If unusually large, grunts may be scaled and filleted, or even baked whole. There are numerous species, differing in appearance, not taste. However, the largest of all—the white margate grunt, which can reach a weight of seven or eight pounds—

tastes very strong when fresh caught, but loses the strong taste after a day or two on ice or a short period of freezing.

HADDOCK. Closely related to the cod, and similar in appearance, haddock may be treated in the same way.

HAKE. Pot-bellied and with a slippery feel, the hake is ignored by many fishermen because of looks. But the meat is white, delicious, almost boneless. Scale and fillet, skin and fillet, or prepare whole for baking.

HALIBUT. See Flatfish.

HOGFISH. Sometimes called hog snapper, though it is not a snapper, the hogfish is thought by many to be the best-tasting fish of warm reefs. Certainly, it would be hard to imagine fish flesh any more fine-grained or pure white. Fillet and skin, then fry, broil or boil. When boiled and served with a bit of salt and melted butter, it tastes much like crab or lobster.

HOUNDFISH. This large needlefish is edible and surprisingly good, either filleted or cut in wide steaks. It can be fried or boiled.

JACK. Incredibly, all the jacks have long had the reputation of being very poor table fare—in the States, at least. Actually, they are among the very best of fish, a fact which isn't yet widely known or accepted. They do require a bit of extra cleaning effort, but not much. After being filleted and skinned, the fillets should be cut in half, *lengthwise*, and the red meat running the length of each piece should be carefully trimmed away—along with some extra bones that lie along that center line. Trimmed fillets may be fried, broiled or boiled for salad. Delicious!

These directions apply to all the jacks, including the jack crevalle, blue runner, bar jack and Almaco or Spanish jack. Perhaps the bar jack is a shade tastier than the others.

KINGFISH. See Mackerel; also Whiting.

LADYFISH. Skip this one. The flesh is, of course, edible, but very soft and very bony.

LING. See Cobia; also Hake.

LINGCOD. See Greenling.

LIZARDFISH. Don't let the ugly looks fool you—as they do most fishermen. The lizardfish has beautiful white flesh and a mild flavor. Scale and prepare as panfish. The odd big ones can be scaled and filleted or filleted and skinned.

LOOKDOWN. Excellent eating and easy to clean. Cut off head and remove entrails, which are in a small pocket just below the gills. Pan-fry whole—or chop in half if you get one too big for your pan. One of the best panfish, the lookdown is similar to pompano.

MACKEREL. Several mackerel species in both the Atlantic and Pacific are similar in table quality. All have oily flesh which is especially well suited to broiling, smoking or salting. Mackerel need not be scaled or skinned. Simply slice off the fillets and broil—or else cut the fillets butterfly-fashion (see Chapter Two) for smoking. Fried mackerel is good, too, and in this case you can skin the fillets. With broiled mackerel, you normally eat the flesh and leave the skin.

Largest of the group is the king mackerel, frequently called kingfish, or king. These generally are steaked, rather than filleted, although small specimens can be treated as regular mackerel. Some of the other mackerel species, particularly the cero of the Atlantic and the sierra of the Pacific, frequently grow large enough to steak.

MARGATE. The white margate of Florida reefs looks exactly like a huge grunt, which indeed it is. See the listing for Grunt. Another species, the black margate, belongs to the same family but is not generally thought of as a grunt because of its large size and dissimilar appearance. The black margate can be scaled and prepared whole for baking, or it can be filleted and skinned for frying or broiling.

MARLIN. Normally, these great game fish of the deep ocean are either mounted or released. When one is brought to dock and escapes the taxidermist, it is usually smoked—and is a real treat. But marlin steaks are also delicious broiled or baked.

MOJARRA. Sometimes called "shad" in South Florida, this is a very good panfish. Scale and prepare whole. Some are large enough to be skinned and filleted.

MOONFISH. See the listing for Lookdown. The moonfish is close to the lookdown in appearance and taste. To make matters more confusing, a lot of people give this name to the lookdown.

MUTTONFISH. See Snapper.

MULLET. The lowly mullet is one of the best-tasting of all fish—very rich and buttery. Eat it soon after catching, or keep it well iced for short periods of time. Because of the oily flesh, poorly-kept mullet become rancid all too quickly. Scale and fillet, then fry or broil. It's also excellent smoked or salted, and the large roe is marvelous. Many mullet are caught by hook-and-line anglers in freshwater rivers, where they are invariably "muddy" tasting. To remove the muddy taste, simply fillet and skin the fish instead of scaling.

PARROT FISH. These grotesque creatures are tricky as table fish—delicious white meat, but the internal organs can be poisonous. Proceed at your own risk, but if you can manage to fillet and skin the fish without cutting into the intestinal area, try boiling the flesh. It tastes like lobster. Also, it can be fried or broiled.

PERCH. This name is incorrectly, but widely, applied to quite a few smallish saltwater fish—especially to the several related types of surf perches or sea perches common everywhere along the Pacific Coast. In the Atlantic, there is the sand perch of southern waters, and some others including the commercially famous "deep sea perch." One true perch of the Atlantic is the white perch, caught in both salt water and in freshwater streams.

There's no need to try separating all these biologically. If a fish wears the name "perch" you can be sure it is an excellent panfish. Scale and prepare whole for pan-frying. Some types do exceed panfish size and can be filleted and skinned or scaled. Usually deep-fried, perch fillets are also good broiled or used in chowder.

PERMIT. When they are small—under seven pounds—it takes a fin-count to distinguish a permit from the common pompano. A cook or gourmet couldn't tell the difference, either. See the listing for Pompano. Large permit—they grow commonly to thirty pounds, and sometimes twice that weight—are also a rare table treat. However, sportsmen play down their appeal in hopes that most folks will release the big ones. A big permit should be filleted and skinned—not an easy job because the fish is very broad. Next, the fillets should be trimmed of dark meat, then sliced into pieces about the size of minute steaks.

And then comes the surprise. Those pieces of permit will taste like the best veal, but of course are much whiter. You can use them in any veal recipe.

PIGFISH. See Grunt.

PINFISH. More often used for bait than for food, pinfish are good panfish. Scale and prepare for pan-frying.

POLLOCK. Strangely, the pollock is not highly regarded as a food fish by anglers, although it is similar to cod in both appearance and taste. The flesh is not nearly so fine-grained as the cod, and this could be a contributing reason. Still, pollock is quite good when filleted and sliced thin for frying or broiling. And probably nobody could tell the difference from cod when the meat is used in chowders or fish cakes.

POMPANO. According to price, pompano is the best fish in the sea, usually served up in fancy dishes like *Almondine* and Pompano *en Papillote*. But there's no need to get fancy. Small pompano, sautéed in a pan, and larger ones baked or broiled can stand on their own as sheer delights—without help from fancy sauces. You needn't scale or skin the fish; simply cut off the head and draw. Fillet, if you prefer. There are several species of pompano, and all are excellent.

PORGY. Here's another panfish favorite which often runs large enough for baking, and is very tasty either way.

Bigger ones often are filleted. Whether to scale or to skin is a personal option. Skinning is much easier.

PORKFISH. A vivid black-and-yellow reef fish related to the grunts, it should be handled the same. See the listing for Grunt.

PUFFER. This heading covers the blowfish or swellfish, and also the rabbitfish or silver puffer. Proceed with caution. All are among the very tastiest fish, having a flavor similar to frog legs and, when marketed commercially in the northeastern states, are frequently labeled "sea chicken." However, certain internal organs of some species of puffer can be very poisonous. Apparently there is nothing to fear from the northern variety of blowfish since, as mentioned, huge quantities of them are consumed. Many people in Florida also relish the southern blowfish and rabbitfish, and cases of poisoning are very rare, though invariably fatal. Despite the fact that careful cleaning and eviscerating, without rupturing any of the entrails, assures a safe and delicious meal, eating the southern forms cannot be recommended here.

RABBITFISH. See Puffer.

RAINBOW RUNNER. A deepwater member of the jack family, this fish is excellent when skinned and trimmed of red meat. Fry or broil.

RAYS. The danger with rays is not in eating them, but in handling. Most have dangerous barbed spikes in the tail. Some can administer an electric shock. Obviously, fishermen don't often bring them home—but the "wings" are very good to eat. Chunks cut from the wings resemble scallops in appearance and flavor.

REDFISH. Also called red drum and channel bass, among other names, this is a popular food fish and a very good one in small sizes. Reds up to seven or eight pounds can be filleted and skinned, then fried, broiled, boiled or baked. Up to twelve pounds or so, they still make fine baking fish, and for this they should be scaled, drawn and beheaded. Trophy-sized redfish are outrageously coarse, and if eaten at all, should be used in chowder or ground for cakes.

ROCKFISH. This name is used for grouper in the Bahamas. See the listing for Grouper. Pacific Coast rockfish species are many, varied—and delicious. Probably more than half the sportsmen's catch in California salt water is made up of rockfish of one species or another. Fillet and skin, and then prepare in any way you prefer.

ROOSTERFISH. Like the jacks, which are close relatives, the roosterfish of Lower California should be filleted and skinned, and trimmed of dark meat. Also like the jack, it's seldom chosen for the table, but quite good.

SAILFISH. If you must bring in a sailfish, by all means smoke it or have it smoked commercially. It can be eaten fresh, but is not nearly so good as many other varieties of fish you can catch in the same waters.

SAILOR'S CHOICE. An excellent panfish, this should be scaled and prepared whole for frying.

SALMON. All salmon found in the sea are also found in freshwater streams. Refer to the Freshwater listings for advice on preparing and cooking.

SAWFISH. When it comes to food fish, beauty is as beauty tastes—but the sawfish is so repugnant-looking that nobody realizes it can be steaked (no need to skin) into one of the best dishes you'll ever get out of the sea. Of course, sawfish are rarely caught, even where they're common, so very few people even get a chance to try the broiled steaks.

SCAD. See Jack.

SCAMP. See Grouper.

SCULPIN. This is a large family, its best-known members being the California rockfish (which see).

SCUP. See Porgy.

SEA ROBIN. Not much meat here, but when skinned and filleted it's darn good. Deep-frying is best.

SHAD. Like the salmon, shad are at home in salt water or fresh—ascending rivers to spawn. See the Freshwater list for guides to cleaning and cooking.

SHARK. Most sharks are edible, some highly prized. Steaks cut from the mako shark are as good as swordfish steaks. The common nurse shark of the South is also a good dinner—again, steaked and broiled. Many sharks, though, have a disagreeably strong taste.

SHEEPSHEAD. Treat as for porgy.

SHEEPSHEAD, CALIFORNIA. A very delicious fish with flaky white flesh. It should be skinned and filleted. Cook it any way you like, but when boiled and served either hot or cold, it tastes much like lobster.

SKATE. Like rays, skates are very good though shunned by most fishermen. Cut chunks of meat from the "wings," and fry, broil or boil.

SKIPJACK. See Tuna.

SMELT. See listing in Freshwater section.

SNAPPER. The name is commonly given to small blue-fish—see that listing. But rightfully the name belongs to a large family of exceptionally fine sport and food fish of the southern Atlantic, southern Pacific and Gulf waters. Best known in the market place is the red snapper. Among many others are (Atlantic) the muttonfish, lane, mangrove, schoolmaster, cubera and yellowtail; and (Lower California) striped, colorado, rose, mullet and yellow snappers. The collective Spanish name is "pargo."

While numerous personal preferences are expressed, all snappers, without exception, are marvelous table fish. Small ones, scaled and prepared whole, can be pan-fried or baked as individual servings. Larger ones are most easily filleted and skinned, unless you wish to bake the whole fish, which is a tasty idea. In that case, scale and draw it and cut off the head. Bake it stuffed or unstuffed. Even the hugest snappers, such as the cubera, are delicious and tender. Skin the giants and cut the meat into slices or large chunks for baking.

SNOOK. This is one of the best southern fish. It yields very thick fillets and should always be filleted and skinned.

Without skinning, it has a soapy taste. Slice the fillets into small pieces, or "fingers," and deep-fry. It's also good broiled or baked, or used in chowder.

SOLE. See Flatfish.

SPADEFISH. See Angelfish.

SPOT. A highly popular panfish. Scale, dress and fry.

SQUIRRELFISH. A good panfish, but difficult to clean and handle, because of wicked gill covers and spines. Since you're bound to catch other good panfish in the same waters, pass it up.

SWORDFISH. The steaks are justly famous, but its popularity as a food fish took a tumble in 1971 when it was removed from the commercial market in the East because of high mercury content. Game fishermen weren't upset because most consider the swordfish the Number One big game prize.

TARPON. The meat is dark and mushy. This fish is never eaten in the States, though in some places it's dried or made into fish cakes.

TALLY, OCEAN. See Triggerfish.

TAUTOG. Also called blackfish, this is a delicious fish which should be filleted and skinned. The white meat then can be fried, boiled or broiled.

TOMCOD. Though not as highly regarded as its larger relative, the cod, the tomcod is just about as good on the table, and can be treated the same way.

TORO. A good panfish. Scale, dress and pan-fry. Or fillet and skin if you have enough of the larger specimens.

TRIGGERFISH. The several varieties of triggerfish, including the beautiful queen trigger and the large ocean tally (sometimes called turbot), are very good and preferred by some over snapper. But they are tough to clean because of the very leathery skin. They can be skinned first, then filleted, or else filleted and then skinned. Either way, take care. You can easily break a thin stainless-steel knife trying to dress a large triggerfish. Worse still, the blade might slip on the rough skin and give you a nasty cut. The fillets can be fried or broiled.

TRIPLETAIL. Odd-looking but fine eating, the tripletail is best filleted and skinned. It can be fried, broiled or baked.

TROUT, SEA. See the listing for Weakfish. Some of the true freshwater trout do run to sea and can be caught along the coast in certain northern areas. See Trout in the Freshwater list.

TUNA. Americans, whether they catch their tuna or buy them in cans, almost invariably express their preferences in terms of the lightest, prettiest meat. Thus the "finest" tuna is the white-meat albacore of the Pacific, and the "worst" are the dark-meat bonitos. Yellowfin, blackfin and small bluefin tuna are happily accepted as "light" compromises. Actually, the dark tuna are said to be the most nutritious and are the preferred species in some parts of the world.

Regardless of all that, any tuna can be boiled and made into a good salad. Fillet, skin and cut it into pieces of desired size. What most fishermen don't know is that pieces of the dark-meat tuna, whether bonito or giant bluefin, can be sautéed or broiled with butter, and taste more like baby beef than fish. And in case you haven't tasted baby beef, it's mild and enjoyable but not as full-flavored as mature beef.

TURBOT. See the listing for Triggerfish. The name also is used for some flounders; see Flatfish.

WAHOO. An excellent offshore game and food fish, similar in appearance and taste to the king mackerel. Best when steaked and broiled, it is also a great fish for smoking.

WEAKFISH. Members of this group are often called "sea trout," and are brothers to the Pacific corbinas and the California white sea bass. Outstanding food fish, they are usually scaled and drawn. Then they can be either filleted or left whole for baking. Along the Gulf Coast, the twelveinchers are frequently dressed whole and served individually, either baked or pan-fried. Usually the head is left on, but this is optional.

WHITING. These are small, slender fish of croaker-like appearance. They're most often scaled, drawn and beheaded, then pan-fried. The flesh is soft. Whiting should be iced immediately after catching. They're also called "kingfish" or "king whiting."

WRASSE. The commonly-caught wrasses are the hogfish, tautog and California sheepshead. See those headings. Most other members of this family are also delicious, with very white and mild flesh.

YELLOWTAIL, ATLANTIC. See Snapper.

YELLOWTAIL, PACIFIC. A California favorite, yellowtail can be either filleted and skinned, or steaked. They're delicious fried, broiled—or just about any way you care to prepare them.

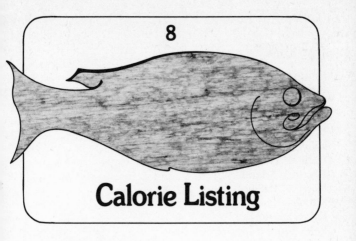

Calorie Listing

All of the following calorie counts are based on 3½-oz. portions of edible food.

We would like to acknowledge and thank the United States Government Printing Office and the Department of Agriculture for all of the data in this list. If you would like a more technical and comprehensive accumulation and breakdown of data we suggest our original source, *Composition of Foods/Agricultural Handbook No. 8*. It may be obtained from the Superintendent of Documents, U.S. Government Printing Office, Washington, D.C. 20402.

	Calories
Abalone	98
Albacore	177
Bass, stuffed	259
Bass, oven/fried	196
Bluefish, baked or broiled	159
Bonito	168
Bullhead	84
Burbot	82
Butterfish, northern	169
Butterfish, gully	95

Catfish	103
Chub	145
Dogfish, spiny	156
Eel	233
Flatfish (Flounder, Sole and Sanddab)	79
Flounder, baked	202
Grouper	87
Haddock, fried	165
Hake	74
Halibut	100
Halibut, Greenland	146
Herring, Atlantic	176
Herring, Pacific	98
Kingfish	105
Lake Herring	96
Lake Trout (approx. 6.5 lbs.)	241
Lingcod	84
Lobster	91
Lobster Newburg	194
Mackerel, broiled in butter	236
Mackerel, salted and smoked	250
Mullet	146
Ocean Perch, Atlantic, fried	227
Ocean Perch, Pacific, fried	283
Octopus	73
Oyster stew	239
Oysters, fried	84
Perch, white	118
Perch, yellow	91
Pollock, cooked	128
Porgy and Scup	112
Red and Gray Snapper	93
Redfish (see Ocean Perch)	
Redhorse, silver	98
Sanddab (see Flatfish)	
Scallops	194
Seabass	96
Shad, baked	201
Sheepshead, Atlantic	113
Shrimp, french-fried	225

140

Sescowet (see Lake Trout)
Skate 98
Smelt 98
Sole (see Flatfish)
Soursop 65
Squid 84
Sturgeon, steamed 160
Suckers, including white 104
Sucket, carp 111
Swordfish, broiled 174
Tautog 89
Tilefish, baked 138
Trout, brook 101
Tuna, bluefin 145
Tuna, yellowfin 133
Tuna salad 170
Whitefish, baked, stuffed 215
Whiting (see Kingfish)
Wreckfish 114
Yellowtail, Pacific 138

141

Index

Abalone, calories in, 139
Albacore tuna, 136
  calories in, 139
Aluminum foil, cooking fish
  with, 82
Amberjack, 121–22
Angelfish, 122
Appetizers, 86–87
  fried fish bits, 87
  seviche, 86
  smoked fish spread, 86–
  87

Bacon, 66, 70
Bags, fish, 3
Baked and baking fish, 65–
  66, 92–99
  alicante, 94
  exotica, 96–97
  fast but fancy, 98–99
  festive, 98
  fillets, Hawaiian, 93–94
  fillets en papillote, 95
  fillets in herb sauce, 97
  fillets with crab and
    shrimp, 95–96
  fillets with sour cream
    and mayonnaise, 98
  frozen, 56
  loaf, 108
  pompano en papillote,
    94–95
  preparation for, 15–19
  recipes, 92–99

Spanish style, 96
  stuffings for, 92–93
Barbecuing fish, 69–72
  smoking, 71–72
Barracuda, 122
Baskets, fish, 3
Bass, 114–15, 122–23
  calories in, 139, 140
  freezing, 48
  rock, 114, 117
  sea, 35–37, 123, 140
  smoked, 74
  stringers for, 2
  striped, 85, 114
Basting fish, 64 66, 70–72
Batter for fried fish, 60
Billfish, butchering, 35–37
Black bass, 114
Black drum, 126
Blowfish, 132
Bluefin tuna, 136
  butchering, 36
  calories in, 141
Bluefish, 123
  broiling, 64
  calories in, 139
  freezing, 48
Bluegill, 117
  filleting, 22–23
  sautéing, 64
Boiled fish, see Poached
  and poaching fish
Bonefish, 124
Boning, shad, 40–43

Bonito, 136
  calories in, 139
Bouillabaisse,
  French, 90–91
  quick, 91
Bouillon, court, 67, 104–5
Bread stuffing, 92–93
Breading fish, 60–61, 79
Bream, 124
Brine solution for smoking,
      71–74
Brine-curing fish, 73–74
Broiled and broiling fish,
      63–64, 101–4
  deviled fillets, 103
  quick and spicy fillets,
      102–3
  recipes, 101–4
  spicy, 102
  steaks, Oriental, 103–4
  steaks au gratin, 101
  steaks au vin, 102
Browning fish, 65
Bruises on fish, 5
Buffalo, 115
Bullhead, calories in, 139
Burbot, calories in, 139
Butchering giant fish, 35–
      37
Butterfish, 124
  calories in, 139
Butterfly fillet (double fil-
      let), 29–30, 72, 80–81

Cabezone, 124
California black bass, 123
California sheepshead, 134
Calorie listing of fish, 139–
      41
Camp stove cooking, 75–78
Campfire cooking of fish,
      80–82
Camping equipment and
      supplies, 76
Carp, 115
  calories in, 141
Cashew nuts, baked fish
      exotica, 96–97
Casserole, creamy flaked
      fish, 110
Catfish, 115, 124
  calories in, 140
  skinning, 37–39
  stew, Southern style, 89

Chain stringers, 2
Charcoal grills, 71–72
Cheese,
  baked fish exotica, 96–97
  broiled steaks au gratin,
      101
  fillets en papillote, 95
Chowders, 87–92
  European, 88–89
  fast, 88
  Manhattan, 91–92
  New England, 87–88
Chub, 115
  calories in, 140
Clams,
  French bouillabaisse, 90–
      91
  quick bouillabaisse, 91
Cleaning and dressing fish,
      6, 7–43
  for baking, large fish,
      15–18
  boning shad, 40–43
  double fillet, 29–30
  filleting and skinning,
      22–28
  filleting extra-large fish,
      31–35
  giant fish, 35–37
  panfish, 9–14
  skinning catfish, 37–39
  steaking, 21–22
  trout and salmon, 19–20
Cobia, 124–25
Cod, 125
  New York stew, 89–90
Cold-storing and freezing
      fish, 45–57
  thawing, 55–56
Cooking equipment,
  camp stoves, 75
  camping, 76
  skillets, 79
  slotted spoons, 61
  smokers, 72–75
  wire-frame broilers, 70,
      72
Cooking fish,
  baking, 65–66, 92–99
  basic methods, 59–83
  broiling, 63–64, 101–4
  on a camp stove, 75–78
  on a campfire, 80–82

fish-fry for large group,
  78–80
frying, 59–62, 87
grilling, 69–71
grill-smoking, 71–72
leftover or flaked, 108–11
outdoors, 69–84
poaching, steaming or
  boiling, 66–67, 104–8
recipes, 85–111
sautéing, 64–65, 99–101
smoking, 71–75
Corbina, 125
Corn flake crumbs, 60
Corn meal, 62–63
Cornbread stuffing, 93
Court bouillon, 67, 104–5
  deluxe, 105
  with wine, 104
Crab,
  baked fillets with shrimp
    and, 95–96
  New York stew, 89–90
  pomano en papillote, 94–
    95
Creels, 5
Croaker, 125
Cunner, 125
Curing fish, 73–74

Dab, 126
Deluxe stew, 90
Deviled broiled fillets, 103
Dogfish, calories in, 140
Dolphin, 125–26
Double fillets, 29–30
  grill-smoking, 72
  planking, 29, 80–81
Dressing fish, 4, 7–43
  for baking, large fish,
    15–18
  boning shad, 40–43
  double fillet, 29–30
  filleting and skinning,
    22–28
  filleting extra-large fish,
    31–35
  giant fish, 35–37
  panfish, 9–14
  skinning catfish, 37–39
  steaking, 21–22
  trout and salmon, 19–20
Drum, 116
  black, 126

Eel, 116
  calories in, 140
Eggs, sautéed smoked fish
  with, 100
Electric grills, 71
Electric hot plates, 73
Equipment, cooking,
  camp stoves, 75
  camping, 76
  skillets, 79
  slotted spoons, 61
  smokers, 72–75
  wire-frame broilers, 70,
    72
Equipment, fishing,
  bags and baskets, 3
  creels, 5
  ice chests, 3–4, 45–46
  knives, 7–8
  scalers, 8, 10, 15
  stringers, 2–3
European chowder, 88–89

Fast chowder, 88
Festive baked fish, 98
Filleted and filleting fish,
  8–9, 22–35
  baked, alicante, 94
  baked, with crab and
    shrimp, 95–96
  baked, fast but fancy,
    98–99
  baked, festive, 98
  baked, Hawaiian, 93–94
  baked, Spanish style, 96
  baked in herb sauce, 97
  baked with sour cream
    and mayonnaise, 98
  baking, 66
  broiling, 63–64
  catfish stew, Southern
    style, 89
  deviled broiled, 103
  double fillet, 29–30, 72,
    80–81
  extra-large fish, 31–35
  for fish-fry, 78
  freezing, 49–50
  frying, 60–62
  grilling outdoors, 70–71
  en papillote, 95
  planking, 29, 80–81
  poached, Hollandaise, 105

145

poached, mariniere, 105–106

poached, supreme, with wine, 107–8

poached trout Normandy, 107

poached with mushrooms, 106

poached with oysters, 106

pompano en papillote, 94–95

quick and spicy broiled, 102–3

rock cooking, 81–82

sautéed in sour cream, 101

sautéing, 64–65

seviche, 86

smoking, 73, 74

spicy broiled, 102

system 1, 22–25

system 2, 26–28

Fish,

bags and baskets for, 3

baked, alicante, 94

baked, exotica, 96–97

baked, fast but fancy, 98–99

baked, festive, 98

baked, Spanish style, 96

bits, fried, 87

cakes, 110–11

calorie listing of, 139–41

chowder, Manhattan, 91–92

cleaning and dressing, 4, 7–43

cold-storing and freezing, 45–57

freshwater guide to, 114–20

loaf, baked, 108

and mushroom pie, 109

Newburg, 108–9

poached, Hollandaise, 105

poached, mariniere, 105–6

poached, with mushrooms, 106

poached, with oysters, 106

poached, supreme, with wine, 107–8

saltwater, guide to, 121–37

sautéed, in sour cream, 101

sautéed smoked, with eggs, 100

spicy broiled, 102

spread, smoked, 86–87

steak, broiled, au vin, 102

steaks, broiled, Oriental, 103–4

stock, 90

see also names of individual fish; names of preparation styles

Fish-fry, planning, 78–80

Fishing,

equipment, 2–5, 7–8

winter, 1

Flaked fish, 108–11

cakes, 110–11

casserole, creamy, 110

loaf, baked, 108

and mushroom pie, 109

Newburg, 108–9

soufflé, 109–10

Flatfish, 126

calories in, 140

Flounder, 126

calories in, 140

freezing, 48

Fluke, 126

Freezer burn, 48, 52

Freezing fish, 45–57

thawing, 56

French bouillabaisse, 90–91

Freshwater fish, guide to, 114–20

Fried fish bits, 87

Frying fish, 59–63

frozen, 56

for large group, 78–80

Gafftopsail catfish, 124

Gas grills, 71

Gray snapper, calories in, 140

Grayling, 116

Greenling, 126–27

Grilling fish outdoors, 69–71

smoking, 71–72

Grouper, 127

146

calories in, 140
freezing, 48
Grunt, 127–28

Haddock, 128
calories in, 140
Hake, 128
calories in, 140
Halibut, 126
calories in, 140
New York stew, 89–90
steaking, 21
Hawaiian baked fillets,
93–94
Heads of fish, 65
Herb sauce, baked fillets
in, 97
Herring, calories in, 140
Hickory sawdust and chips,
71, 74
Hogfish, 128
Hollandaise, poached fish,
105
Hot plates, electric, 73
Houndfish, 128
Hush puppies, 62–63, 77,
78–79

Ice chests, 3–4, 45–46
Ice fishing, 1

Jack, 128

Kelp bass, 123
King mackerel (kingfish),
129
calories in, 140
steaking, 21
Kingfish (whiting), 137
basting, 70
calories in, 141
Knives, 7–8

Ladyfish, 128
Lake herring, calories in,
140
Largemouth bass, 114
smoked, 74
Leftover fish, 108–11
Lingcod, 127
calories in, 140
Live-wells, 3
Lizardfish, 129

Loaf, baked fish, 108
Lobster,
calories in, 140
French bouillabaisse,
90–91
Lookdown, 129

Mackerel, 129
broiling, 64
calories in, 140
freezing, 48
steaking, 21
Mako shark, 36, 134
Mangrove snapper, filleting,
23
Manhattan fish chowder,
91–92
Margate, 129
Marinate for smoking,
71–74
Marlin, 36, 129
Mayonnaise, baked fillets
with sour cream and,
98
Mojarra, 130
Moonfish, 130
Mullet, 130
calories in, 140
freezing, 48
Mushrooms,
and fish pie, 109
poached fish with, 106
and rice stuffing, 92
Muskellunge, 116, 117

New England chowder,
87–88
New York stew, 89–90
Newburg, fish, 108–9
Northern pike, 118
Nurse shark, 134

Octopus, calories in, 140
Oriental broiled fish steaks,
103–4
Outdoor cooking, 69–84
Oysters,
calories in, 140
French bouillabaisse,
90–91
poached fish with, 106

Pacific yellowtail, 137
Pan broiled fish, *see*

Sautéed and sautéing
  fish
Pan fried fish, *see* Sautéed
  and sautéing fish
Panfish, 116–17
  dressing, 9–14
  eating, 82–84
  for fish-fry, 78
  freezing, 48, 50
  knives for cleaning, 8
Parrot fish, 130
Peanut oil, 61
Pepper, 61–62
Perch, 117, 130
  calories in, 140
Permit, 131
Pickerel, 117
Pie, fish and mushroom,
  109.
Pike, 118
  northern, 118
  redfin, 118
Pineapple, baked fillets
  Hawaiian, 93–94
Pinfish, 131
Planking fish, 29, 80–81
Pliers, 8
Poached and poaching fish,
  66–67, 104–8
  Hollandaise, 105
  mariniere, 105–6
  with mushrooms, 106
  with oysters, 106
  recipes, 104–8
  supreme, with wine,
    107–8
  trout Normandy, 107
Pollock, 131
  calories in, 140
Pomano, 131
  en papillote, 94–95
Porgy, 131–32
  calories in, 140
Porkfish, 132
Potatoes,
  creamy flaked fish
    casserole, 110
  fast chowder, 88
  fish cakes, 110–11
  New England chowder,
    87–88
  poached fish supreme,
    with wine, 107–8
Puffer, 132

Quick and spicy broiled
  fillets, 102–3
Quick bouillabaisse, 91

Rabbitfish, 132
Rainbow runner, 132
Ray, 132
Red snapper, 85, 134
  calories in, 140
Redfin pike, 118
Redfish, 132
Redhorse, calories in, 140
Refrigerating fish, 47
Rice-mushroom stuffing, 92
  baked fillets Hawaiian,
    93–94
Rock bass, 114, 117
Rockfish, 133
Rocks, cooking with, 81–82
Roosterfish, 133
Russian style sautéed
  trout, 100

Sailfish, 36, 133
  smoked, 74
Sailor's choice, 133
Salmon, 118–19
  basting, 70
  dressing, 19–20
  fishing for, 2, 4–5
  freezing, 48
  poached, Normandy, 107
  poached, supreme, with
    wine, 107–8
  poaching, 67
  smoked, 74
  steaking, 21
Salt, 61–62
Saltwater fish, guide to,
  121–37
Sanddab, calories in, 140
Sauger, 119
Sautéed and sautéing fish,
  64–65, 99–101
  amandine, 99
  amandine, spicy, 99–100
  recipes, 99–101
  smoked with eggs, 100
  in sour cream, 101
  trout, Russian style, 100
Sawfish, 133
Scalers, 8, 10, 15
Scaling fish, 8, 10, 15

148

Scallops,
  calories in, 140
  French bouillabaisse,
    90–91
Sculpin, 133
Scup, calories in, 140
Sea bass, 123
  calories in, 140
  giant, butchering, 35–37
Sea robin, 133
Sea trout, 125, 136–37
Seviche, 86
Shad, 118, 134
  boning, 40–43
  calories in, 140
Shark, 134
  butchering, 35–37
  mako, 36, 134
Sharpening stone, 8
Sheepshead, 134
  calories in, 141
Shellcracker, 117
Shipping fish, 56–57
Shrimp,
  baked fillets with crab
    and, 95–96
  calories in, 141
  French bouillabaisse,
    90–91
  New York stew, 89–90
  poached trout Normandy,
    107
  pompano en papillote,
    94–95
  quick bouillabaisse, 91
Skate, 134
  calories in, 141
Skillets, 79
Skinning fish, 22–28
  catfish, 37–39
  extra-large fish, 31
Slotted spoons, 61
Smallmouth bass, 114
Smelt, 119–20
  calories in, 141
Smoked and smoking fish,
    72–75
  grilling, 71–72
  sautéed with eggs, 100
  smokers for fish, 72–75
  spread, 86–87
Snapper, 134
  broiling, 64
  filleting, 23

mangrove, 23
red, 85, 134, 140
Snook, 135
  freezing, 48
Sole, 126
  calories in, 140
  poached, mariniere,
    105–6
  pompano en papillote,
    94–95
Soufflé, flaked fish, 109–10
Soups, 87–92
  catfish stew, Southern
    style, 89
  deluxe stew, 90
  European chowder,
    88–89
  fast chowder, 88
  French bouillabaisse,
    90–91
  Manhattan fish chowder,
    91–92
  New England chowder,
    87–88
  New York stew, 89–90
  quick bouillabaisse, 91
  stock, fish, 90
Sour cream,
  baked fillets with mayon-
    naise and, 98
  sautéed fish in, 101
  stuffing, 93
Soursop, calories in, 141
Southern style catfish stew,
    89
Spanish style baked fish,
    96
Spicy broiled fish, 102
Spicy sauté amandine,
    99–100
Spot, 135
Spread, smoked fish, 86–87
Squawfish, 119–20
Squid, calories in, 141
Squirrelfish, 135
Steaked and steaking fish,
    21–22
  baked, alicante, 94
  baked, fast but fancy,
    98–99
  baking, 66
  broiled, Oriental, 103–4
  broiled au gratin, 101
  broiled au vin, 102

149

broiling, 63–64
for fish-fry, 78
freezing, 50
grilling outdoors, 70–71
poached, supreme with
wine, 107–8
poaching, 67
sautéed in sour cream,
101
smoking, 73
Steamed fish, *see* Poached
and poaching fish
Stews, 87, 89–91
catfish, Southern style, 89
deluxe, 90
French bouillabaisse,
90–91
New York, 89–90
quick bouillabaisse, 91
Stock, fish, 90
Storing fish, 45–57
shipping and transport-
ing, 56–57
thawing, 55–56
Stringers, 2–3
Striped bass, 85, 114
Stuffed fish, grill-smoking,
72
Stuffings,
bread, 92–93
cornbread, 93
rice-mushroom, 91
sour cream, 93
Sturgeon, 120
calories in, 141
smoked, 74
Sucker, 120
calories in, 141
Sucket, calories in, 141
Sunfish, 116–17
filleting, 23
Swordfish, 135
butchering, 36
calories in, 141
steaking, 21, 36

Tarpon, 135
Tautog, 135
calories in, 141
Thawing frozen fish, 55–56
Tilefish, calories in, 141
Tomcod, 135
Toro, 135
Transporting fish, 56–57

Triggerfish, 135–36
Tripletail, 136
Trout, 120–21
calories in, 140, 141
dressing, 19–20
fishing for, 2, 4–5
freezing, 48
knives for cleaning, 8
poached, Normandy, 107
poached, supreme, with
wine, 107–8
poaching, 67
sautéed, Russian style,
100
sautéing, 64
sea, 136–37
Tuna, 136
albacore, 136, 139
bluefin, 36, 136, 141
bonito, 136, 139
calories in, 139, 141
freezing, 48
poaching, 67
Turbot, 135–36

Wahoo, 136
Walleye, 85
Warmouth, 117
Weakfish, 125, 136–37
White bass, 114
White sea bass, 122
Whitefish, 121
calories in, 141
Whiting, 137
calories in, 141
see also Kingfish
Wine,
broiled fish au vin, 102
court bouillon deluxe,
105
court bouillon with, 104
poached fish supreme,
with, 107–8
Winter fishing, 1
Wire-frame broilers, 70, 72
Wrapping fish, 51–55
Wrasse, 137
Wreckfish, calories in, 141

Yellow bass, 115
Yellowfin tuna, 136
calories in, 139
Yellowtail, 137
calories in, 141